Canto is an imprint offering a range of titles, classic and more recent, across a broad spectrum of subject areas and interests. History, literature, biography, archaeology, politics, religion, psychology, philosophy and science are all represented in Canto's specially selected list of titles, which now offers some of the best and most accessible of Cambridge publishing to a wider readership.

The Christianisation of the Roman world lies at the root of modern Europe, yet at the time it was a tentative and piecemeal process. Peter Brown's study examines the factors which proved decisive and the compromises which made the emergence of the Christian 'thought world' possible. He shows how contemporary narratives wavered between declarations of definitive victory and a sombre sense of the strength of the pre-Christian past, reflecting the hopes and fears of different generations faced with different social and political situations. He examines the social factors which muted the sharp intolerance which pervades the contemporary literary evidence, and he shows how Christian holy men were less representatives of a triumphant and intransigent faith than negotiators, at ground level, of a working compromise between the new faith and traditional ways of dealing with the supernatural world. His illuminating analysis of religious change as the art of the possible has a wide relevance for other periods and regions.

AUTHORITY AND THE SACRED

AUTHORITY

AND THE SACRED

Aspects of the Christianisation
of the Roman world

PETER BROWN
Princeton University

Published by the Press Syndicate of the University of Cambridge
The Pitt Building, Trumpington Street, Cambridge CB2 1RP
40 West 20th Street, New York, NY 10011–4211, USA
10 Stamford Road, Oakleigh, Melbourne 3166, Australia

© Cambridge University Press 1995

First published 1995
Reprinted 1996 twice
Canto edition 1997

A catalogue record for this book is available from the British Library

Library of Congress cataloguing in publication data
Brown, Peter Robert Lamont.
Authority and the sacred: aspects of the Christianisation of the
Roman world / Peter Brown
p. cm.
Includes bibliographical references and index.
ISBN 0 521 49557 1 (hardback) – ISBN 0 521 59557 6 (paperback)
1. Church history – Primitive and early church, *c.* 30–600.
2. Rome – Religion. 1. Title.
BR170.B72 1992 270.1–dc20 94–42652 CIP

ISBN 0 521 49557 1 hardback
ISBN 0 521 59557 6 paperback

Transferred to digital printing 2002

WD

Contents

Preface

These three chapters are a version of lectures delivered at Cambridge on 22, 23 and 24 November 1993. The occasion was organised at Clare Hall by Dr Janet Huskinson with unfailing thoughtfulness. It was rendered gracious by the hospitality and by the participation throughout of the President, Sir Anthony Low. The panel of discussants chaired by Keith Hopkins – Peter Garnsey, Robin Lane Fox, Christopher Kelly and Rosamond McKitterick – have not only left me with food for thought for many years to come: they provided us all with a model, for our times, of commentary and disagreement that were as lively as they were courteous. The presence in the audience of so many friends and colleagues – Henry Chadwick, Ian Wood, Robert Markus, William Frend, Andrew Palmer, to mention only a few – guaranteed that the discussion ranged vigorously throughout the entire late Roman and early medieval period. Altogether, I present these chapters with a touch of sadness: they are, simply, the lees of the wine – what survives in print of an unusually vivid and humane occasion.

A shorter version of the first chapter had been delivered, in the previous year, as a Raleigh lecture of the British Academy (Peter Brown, 'The Problem of Christianisation', *Proceedings of the*

British Academy: 1992 Lectures and Memoirs 82 (1993), pp. 89–106).
The themes of that chapter, and of the two subsequent chapters,
emerged in large part as a result of my work for sections of
volumes XIII and XIV of the *Cambridge Ancient History*. I owe
much to my *ergodiôktés* in this venture, Averil Cameron, who,
along with her editorial colleagues, has done nothing less than
place, at long last, three whole centuries of the later Roman period
in their rightful place, at the culmination of the history of the
ancient world. I was saddened that illness prevented her from
acting as a discussant of work in which she has been a continuous,
inspiring presence.

I trust that these chapters speak for themselves without
extensive introduction. The reader, however, should be careful to
bear in mind that this book is, indeed, a study of *aspects*, only, of
the Christianisation of the Roman world. The chapters are narrow
flakes, struck from the immense block of an event that lies at the
root of much of the religion and culture of modern Europe. I have
concentrated on 'aspects', in this manner, not simply out of
academic caution. It is because I have long suspected that accounts
of the Christianisation of the Roman world are at their most
misleading when they speak of that process as if it were a single
block, capable of a single comprehensive description, that, in turn,
implies the possibility of a single, all-embracing explanation.

A modern historian of the rise of Christianity in the Roman
world does not have to repeat the facilitating simplifications of
those who were contemporary to that process. Faced by the rapid
changes that followed the conversion of Constantine, in 312,
Christians and pagans alike needed to generate explanatory
narratives that made sense of success, on the one side, and
eventual failure, on the other. My first chapter is devoted to a
dominant narrative of Christianisation, that circulated widely in
Christian circles in the fourth and fifth centuries. It examines the

social circumstances and the slow changes of mentality by which this dominant narrative came to be flanked, in the Latin world, by a considerably less euphoric attitude – by a view of Christianisation that was prepared to linger less on the supernatural triumph of Christ and more on the weight of the pagan past within the Christian present.

In chapter two, I touch on a narrative generated by Christians and pagans alike, that has achieved unquestionable status as if it were a commonsensical statement of the obvious. It is universally assumed, first, that the laws of Christian emperors played a decisive role in ensuring the victory of the Church over all its rivals, and, second, that this was only to be expected: that the late Roman period, as a whole, was overshadowed by the rise of religious intolerance, and that the end of the fourth century, in particular, was characterised by widespread and decisive outbreaks of violence, on the part of Christians, against Jews and pagans. In this chapter, I have no wish to deny this clearly documented streak in late Roman history. I do, however, wish to set the vivid certainties of many Christian texts against a wider background. For these certainties, loudly though they came to echo in later centuries of the Christian middle ages, were dwarfed and muffled, at the time, by the long habits of an upper-class society, whose members maintained a sure sense of politics as the art of the possible, a reluctance to see their social world in terms of mutually exclusive, confessional categories, and that retained a certain merciful *pudeur* when it came to outright acts of religious victimisation and religious violence.

No-one is more aware than I am myself that this chapter is only a beginning. It points the way to a subject which was not exhausted by the discussion subsequent to the lectures. For once we weaken the persuasive power of one, obvious narrative of Christianisation in the Roman empire – the unholy alliance between authoritarian legislation and a triumphant groundswell of Christian intolerance – we have only displaced the problem, not resolved it. Instead, a gentle violence should be seen to have been brought to bear in more subtle, less melodramatic ways, more widely diffused throughout society. We still have to ask what were the vectors of the change, that caused a whole society from Europe to the Middle East to identify the stability of its social order with the spread of a novel and exclusive religion. Whatever the answer to that question may prove to be, I suspect that it will come only if we are prepared to look beyond the stridently self-confident Roman empire of the fourth and early fifth centuries, the empire that produced the *Theodosian Code*. We must venture deep into the less certain centuries of the early middle ages. The differing vicissitudes of state-power, and its relationship to religious authority, along a whole spectrum of societies, from the emergent states of the West, through Byzantium, to the Christian kingdoms of Armenia, Georgia and Ethiopia, must be studied, in order to provide an explanation of the eventual identification of Christianity with authority, that is the hallmark of the medieval world.

Hence, my third chapter attempts to look beyond the vivid image of a well-known figure of Christian late antiquity – the Christian holy man. Having lingered, for many decades now, with delight and constant profit, on the *Lives* of the great saints of Byzantium and the Latin West, I decided that the time had come for me to learn how to use these texts to recover the story that they were written, in large part, to eclipse. I attempt, in this chapter, to glimpse, out of the corner of the eye, as it were, of these *Lives*, the vast, muted landscape of pre-Christian belief and practice against which the activities of holy men took place. I wish to use the bright technicolour of their narratives to find my way to a grey time between the gods, when pagan practice had been prohibited and when Christianity itself, though officially triumphant, was by no means, as yet, the religion of the 'cognitive majority' among the populations of Europe and the Middle East.

If the reader of these three chapters comes away with a greater sense of how much more still needs to be done on the problem of Christianisation in the entire first millennium AD, then these lectures will have been of some use. May they help to encourage further debates as vigorous, and, I trust, as generous, as those which took place, to my delight, in Cambridge in November 1993.

Chapter 1

CHRISTIANISATION
narratives and processes

FACED BY A TOPIC AS LABYRINTHINE AS THE PROBLEM OF
Christianisation, it is a relief to begin with a person for whom the
problem apparently caused little trouble. Some time in fourth
century Britain, Annianus, son of Matutina, had a purse of
six silver pieces stolen from him. He placed a leaden curse in
the sacred spring of Sulis Minerva at Bath, in order to bring
the miscreant to the attention of the goddess. On this tablet, the
traditional list of antithetical categories, that would constitute an
exhaustive description of all possible suspects – 'whether man or
woman, boy or girl, slave or free' – begins with a new antithesis:
seu gentilis seu christianus quaecumque, 'whether a gentile or a
Christian, whomsoever'. As Roger Tomlin, the alert editor of the
tablets, has observed: 'it is tempting to think that a novel
gentilis/christianus pair was added as a tribute to the universal
power of Sulis'.[1] Christianisation, at the shrine of Sulis Minerva at
Bath, means knowledge of yet another world-wide category of
persons whose deeds were open to the eye of an effective goddess
of the post-Constantinian age.

Annianus, and many other fourth-century persons, lived in a
universe rustling with the presence of many divine beings. In that
universe, Christians, even the power of Christ and of his servants,

the martyrs, had come to stay. But they appear in a perspective to which our modern eyes take some time to adjust – they are set in an ancient, pre-Christian spiritual landscape.

What has to be explained is why these hints of the infinitely diverse religious world of the fourth century remain what they are for any modern reader – tantalising fragments, glimpsed through the chinks of a body of evidence which claims to tell a very different story. It is this story to which we are accustomed. Put briefly: the notion that a relatively short period (from the conversion of Constantine, in 312, to the death of Theodosius II, in 450) witnessed the 'end of paganism'; the concomitant notion that the end of paganism was the natural consequence of a long-prepared 'triumph of monotheism' in the Roman world; and the tendency to present the fourth century AD as a period over-shadowed by the conflict between Christianity and paganism – all this amounts to a 'representation' of the religious history of the age that was first constructed by a brilliant generation of Christian historians, polemicists and preachers in the opening decades of the fifth century.[2] By means of this representation, Christian writers imposed (with seemingly irrevocable success, to judge by most modern accounts of the period) a firm narrative closure on what had been, in reality, in the well-chosen words of Pierre Chuvin, a 'Wavering Century'.[3]

Yet, rather than regret this fact, we should look for a moment at why an articulate body of Christian opinion should have chosen to see the history of their own times in this particular manner. It provided for them a facilitating narrative. It was a narrative that held in suspense precisely what we would now call the 'problem of Christianisation'.

In the first place, we must remember the extent to which the conflict between Christianity and paganism was presented, in fourth- and fifth-century Christian sources, as having been fought out in heaven rather than on earth. The end of paganism occurred with the coming of Christ to earth. It was when He was raised on the Cross on Calvary – and not, as we more pedestrian historians tend to suppose, in the reign of Theodosius I – that heaven and earth rang with the crash of falling temples.[4] The alliance of the Christian church with Christian emperors, to abolish sacrifice and to close and destroy the temples, was no more than a last, brisk mopping-up operation, that made manifest on earth a victory already won, centuries before, by Christ, over the shadowy empire of the demons.

It was, indeed, the starkly supernatural quality of this narrative that made it so useful to contemporaries. It suspended the sense of time. Not only was the triumph of Christ preordained: each manifestation of it was instantaneous. As a result, the immediate human consequences of that victory could be taken for granted. The gods were thought to have passed away from whole regions much as, in the Christian rite of exorcism, the demon was believed to have passed out of the body of the possessed in a single, dramatic spasm, that left the sufferer free to return, immediately, to normal health of mind and body. Narratives of the end of paganism – such as the dramatic destruction of the Serapeum of Alexandria in around 392 – follow an analogous, brisk rhythm.[5] It was enough that Serapis should be seen to have been driven from the shrine that he had 'possessed' for so many centuries, by the power of Christ, made palpable through the successful violence of His servants. It was assumed that Alexandria had been 'healed' by the passing of its greatest god, and could henceforth be treated as a Christian city.

More important still, such an otherworldly narrative even enabled the devotees of the old gods to accept what was, often, a brutal *fait accompli*. The worshippers of Serapis declared that, in a manner characteristic of the gods of Egypt, their god had simply withdrawn to heaven, saddened that so much blasphemy should happen in his favoured city.[6] The end of sacrifice and the closing of the temples merely reflected on earth the outcome of a conflict of mighty invisible beings. The acclaimed triumph of the one and the lordly withdrawal of the other had to be accepted by mere mortals. No further questions needed to be asked, and life could resume as usual in a murmurous city. Even the defeated had been given a slender imaginative basis for accommodation to the new regime, in much the same way as the solemn, public *psychodrame* of the *damnatio memoriae* of usurpers both declared the notional, eternal victory of the rightful emperor, and, so it was hoped, brought to a merciful close the potentially murderous lacerations of prolonged civil war.

It is, however, in its modern, laicised form that the fifth-century Christian 'representation' of their times has come to influence our own approach to the problem of Christianisation. As a result of a body of late antique Christian evidence largely intended to give a satisfying sense of narrative pace and direction to the progressive triumph of the Church, the process of Christianisation has tended to be presented largely in terms of the impact of a formidable moving body upon the inert and static mass of ancient paganism.[7]

We are like little boys on the sea-shore. We watch with fascinated delight as the tide sweeps in upon an intricate sand-castle. We note when each segment crumbles before the advancing waters. Some parts fall quickly. They have well-known dates: 384, for the controversy on the removal of the Altar of Victory from the Roman Senate-House; 392 (perhaps), for the destruction of the Serapeum; 529, for the closing of the Academy at Athens. Others provoke a sigh only in the erudite: on 24 August 394, for instance, we say good-bye to our last Egyptian hieroglyph.[8] Nothing thrills us more than to find parts of the sandcastle that have escaped the oncoming tide. We experience an understandable moment of vertigo when Carlo Ginzburg tells us, in his *Storia notturna*, about the old ladies of the Val di Fassa, who informed none other than Nicholas Cusanus, at Bressanone in 1457, that they had touched the shaggy, bear-paw hands of *La Richella*, 'the mother of all wealth and good fortune' – a Braurian Artemis (for Ginzburg, at least) still ministering to the mountain villages of the Alps.[9]

Altogether, we tend to approach the problem of Christianisation as a matter of charting the impact of Christian belief and practice on the whole range of late antique religion and society. We tend to ask, 'What difference did Christianity make?'[10] Unlike our fifth-century predecessors, of course, we do not have the same high expectations of success. The lie of the land of an ancient Mediterranean society makes it seem unlikely to us that all but the most exposed and seaward parts of the sandcastle should fall. We assume that the unthinking mass of *hommes moyens sensuels* could never have been deeply affected by the icy tide of a doctrinaire Christianity – by its shrill ascetic denunciations of sexual pleasure, much less by its Utopian utterances on wealth, slavery and warfare – whose spluttering foam fills so many volumes of the *Patrologia*, as it swashed ineffectually around the solid high ground of Roman *mores*. Christianisation, if it happened at all, must be a slow process, doomed to incompleteness. As Robin Lane Fox has warned us, in the opening pages of his vivid book, *Pagans and Christians*, the brilliant reign of Constantine 'was only a landmark in the history of Christianisation, that state which is always receding, like full employment or a garden without weeds'.[11]

I would like to step aside from this way of looking at the problem of Christianisation. Instead, I will turn, first, to the heavens – to evoke a deeply rooted collective representation of the universe, which gave late antique persons the intellectual and imaginative tools with which to grapple with the ambiguous religious situation of their age. Second, I will return firmly to earth – to suggest that this particular representation owed its tenacity, in the fourth and early fifth centuries, in large part to the manner in which it lent cosmic validation to the rapid and, for a time at least, self-confident emergence of a new style of imperial rule and a new *ethos* of upper-class life. Third, to conclude, I will sketch the manner in which a crisis of confidence in the imperial system, which became increasingly apparent in the Western empire of the late fourth century, was compounded by a regrouping of Christian opinion, in such a way as to lead to the emergence of an alternative representation of the process of Christianisation to the one we described at the beginning of this chapter. Through the works of Saint Augustine, its more sobre, less vibrantly triumphant and supernatural tones would come to exercise a profound influence on the manner in which Western Christians would look back on the triumph of the Church in the Roman world.

Let us first look up to the heavens. We must remember that it is not easy to do so. Living as we do in a bleakly submonotheistic age, we tend to look up into the sky and to find it empty. We no longer see there a *mundus*, a physical universe as heavy as a swollen cloud (for good or ill) with the presence of invisible beings. Belief in an everlasting universe, at once inhabited and governed by intertwined hierarchies of divine beings and their ethereal ministers, was an article of faith for most late classical persons.[12] It had been put at risk by the rise of Christian doctrine on the Creation and on the end of the world: *vigentem . . . aeternitate sua mundum velut temporarium brevemque despiciunt*; 'The *mundus*, the visible universe, pulsing with the energy of life eternal, they despise, as time-bound and of brief duration'.[13]

It is this collective representation of the divine world that we must first install in the back of our minds when we read the late antique evidence. If we do not do so, this evidence will appear to us as crisp and as clear-cut, but as unreal, as a lunar landscape from which the subtle shades imparted by an atmosphere have been drained. Of all the collective representations that had to move, through the slow redrawing of the map of the divine world at the behest of Christian theologians and preachers, the ancient representation of the *mundus* was the one which shifted with the slowness of a glacier.

Contemporaries tended to stress, in practice, the supernatural compartmentalisation of the universe at the expense of its notional unity. The highest divine power was thought to inhabit its shining upper reaches, far beyond the solid brilliance of the stars. Human beings, placed on an earth that lay in the 'sump-hole of the universe',[14] enjoyed the benevolence of that high power largely through a host of lower spirits, who brushed the earth with their ministrations. An imaginative structure of such ancient majesty and self-evident truth constituted the religious common sense of large numbers of fourth-century persons. It was a common sense shared by Christians. Listen to Saint Augustine preaching in Carthage:

> There are those who say: 'God is good, he is great, supreme, eternal and inviolable. It is He who will give us eternal life and that incorruption which He promised as the resurrection. But these things of the physical world and of our present time (*ista vero saecularia et temporalia*) belong to the *daemones* and to the invisible Powers.'
>
> They leave aside God, as if these things did not belong to Him; and by sacrifices, by all kinds of healing devices, and by the expert counsel of their fellows . . . they seek out ways to cope with what concerns this present life.[15]

It was further assumed that the favoured servants of the One High God were those best informed, also, about the turbulent lower reaches of the *mundus*. They could be trusted to give advice on how to achieve health and happiness in this world. In the 420s, Shenoute of Atripe observed that a provincial governor, 'a man with a reputation for being wise', had taken to wearing a jackal's claw tied to his right toe. The governor informed him that he did this on the recommendation ' of a certain Great Monk'.[16] A leading Christian ascetic had validated what appeared to Shenoute to be a blatantly non-Christian occult remedy.

Shenoute's reaction is interesting. Faced by the thoughtful governor, he did not think of denying the existence of a universe sharply divided between upper and lower powers. He countered, rather, with an exaltation of the power of Christ, as the one being Who was uniquely able to bridge the imaginative fissure that ran across the universe, separating its highest from its lowest reaches. The power of Christ was able to reach down to touch all aspects of daily life in the material world.

> Try to attain to the full measure of this Name, and you will find it on your mouth and on the mouths of your children. When you make high festival and when you rejoice, cry Jesus. When anxious and in pain, cry Jesus. When little boys and girls are laughing, let them cry Jesus. And those who flee before barbarians, cry Jesus. And those who go down to the Nile, cry Jesus. And those who see wild beasts and sights of terror, cry Jesus. Those who are taken off to prison, cry Jesus. And those whose trial has been corrupted and who receive injustice, cry the Name of Jesus.[17]

For men such as Augustine and Shenoute, in the opening decades of the fifth century, the 'Christianisation' that mattered most was the imaginative Christianisation of the *mundus* – the consequential assertion of its unity, as subject to the exclusive power of the One God, revealed to the world through Jesus Christ, in the face of an ancient, more compartmentalised model, that had tended to explain, and, hence, to excuse, the observed diversity of religious practice on earth. It meant nothing less than the creation of a religious common sense about the actions of the divine and the nature of the universe different from that held by the 'cognitive majority' of their fellows.

The creation of a new religious 'common sense' is a weighty matter, and in order to approach it we must return from heaven to earth – more precisely, to the age of Constantine and his successors, to the fourth-century Roman empire, before the changes that marked its last decades.

When we turn to the public culture of the fourth century, we are faced by a series of apparent disjunctions that force us to re-think what we mean by 'Christianisation' in this period. The situation is as follows. In the fourth century AD, there were many well-placed inhabitants of the restored Roman empire who would have agreed with Professor Clifford Geertz, that 'At the political center of any complexly organized society . . . there is both a governing elite and a set of symbolic forms expressing the fact that it is in truth governing.'[18] Yet a glance at the art and secular culture of the later empire makes one fact abundantly clear; when the 'governing elite' of this officially Christian empire presented themselves to themselves and to the world at large, as being 'in truth governing', the 'set of symbolic forms' by which they expressed this fact owed little or nothing to Christianity.

The array of symbolic forms by which the *potentes* of the later empire showed their dominance was impressive. Hauntingly post-classical mosaics adorned their villas.[19] Exuberant adaptations of old rituals celebrated their power and prosperity.[20] An elaboration of ceremonial characterised the imperial court.[21] Styles of poetry, of letter-writing and of rhetoric flourished, with which to express the solidarity of the governing class and to act as emblems of their authority.[22] The drastic rearrangement of so many classical traditions in order to create a whole new heraldry of power was one of the greatest achievements of the late Roman period. Yet, it would be profoundly misleading to claim that changes in this large area of social and cultural life reflected in any way a process of 'Christianisation'. What matters, in fact, is the exact opposite. We are witnessing the vigorous flowering of a public culture that Christians and non-Christians alike could share.

The distinctive flavour of fourth-century upper-class life is shown most vividly in its artefacts. Take the *de luxe* manuscript of a *Calendar* presented in 354 to a well-to-do person, Valentinus. It was prepared by an artist who later worked for Pope Damasus and may even have executed commissions for the elder Melania[23] – that formidable ascetic lady, pilgrim to the Holy Land and patroness of Saint Jerome's youthful friend, Rufinus. It bore an acceptable, post-Constantinian acclamation, *Floreas in Deo*; and it contained a list of the festivals of the Roman Church, and the commemorative dates for the burials of leading popes. Yet the illustrated sections of the *Calendar* consist of lovingly circum-stantial representations of those rites of the Roman public cult associated with each month. In the words of the title of Michele Salzman's new book on the *Calendar of 354*, Valentinus, the Christian aristocrat, was still a man who lived *On Roman Time*.[24]

Yet it would be unhelpful to ask which part of the *Calendar* was 'real' and which an empty shell, maintained only by unthinking tradition. The more we look at such art, the more we are impressed by the way in which the parts that we tend to keep in separate compartments, by labelling them 'classical', even 'pagan', as distinct from 'Christian', form a coherent whole; they sidle up to each other, under the subterranean attraction of deep homologies.[25] The classical and Christian elements are not simply incompatible, nor can their relative degree of presence or absence be taken as an indicator of a process of Christianisation – by which standard, Valentinus, the Roman, would, perhaps, be deemed to have barely made it to the half-way post. Rather, the classical elements have been redeployed. They are often grouped in such a way as to convey, if anything, an even heavier charge of meaning. The gods make their appearance, now, as imposing emblems of power and prosperity. Their haunting sensuousness, the quiet majesty that their presence imparts to scenes of abundance and repose, their postclassical, pudgy playfulness, bring down a touch of the opulence of a *mundus*, whose lower reaches, peopled still by the guardians of earthly things – of victory, of love, of the fruits of the earth – had not yet paled beneath the presence of the One God. They added a numinous third dimension to the solidity of a *saeculum* restored to order by Constantine and his successors.[26]

It is not enough to say of these representations, as Hegel later did of the statues of the gods in modern times, *unser Knie beugen wir doch nicht mehr*, 'but we no longer bend the knee'.[27] For, in the fourth century, such fragments appear precisely in those places where men did bend the knee – if not to the ancient gods, at least to other men, to the emperor and to the powerful, for whom *adoratio*, full-blooded reverence, was deemed an utterly appropriate gesture.[28]

Even the symbols of the new, Christian dispensation – the Christogram, the *labarum*, a little later, exquisite ornamental crosses – appear in places allotted to them by the common celebration of the *reparatio saeculi*, of the *felicitas saeculi*, of a world restored and at ease, despite potential chaos. They appear on almost any significant or prestigious object connected with the new elites – on milestones, on mosaic pavements, on sets of luxury cutlery, even, indeed, on the iron dog-collar of a slave, with the inscription, 'Arrest me, for I have run away, and bring me back to the Mons Caelius, to the palace of Elpidius, *vir clarissimus.*'[29]

The mysterious – and now notorious – hoard of silverware known as the Sevso Treasure makes this plain. Here we meet a beneficiary of the Christian empire – a provincial aristocrat, maybe a military man of non-Roman origin – who lived well, hunting with his favourite horse, Innocentius, and feeding on the delicious freshwater fish unique to Lake Balaton. Sevso was there to stay: in the words of the inscription placed around the hunting scene on his main serving plate – a mere 6 pounds of solid silver,

> May these, O Sevso, yours for many ages be,
> Small vessels fit to serve your offspring worthily.[30]

Christianity, also, was there to stay: the *labarum* appears at the beginning of the inscription, directly above the central figure, as he reclines at his ease in the huntsman's banquet. Like the little scenes of the emperors sacrificing to the gods, that were once turned out from cake-moulds, associated with public banquets in second-century Britain and Pannonia, the *labarum* now made formidably familiar, in the same province, the supernatural power under whose distant protection the *saeculum* had, for a moment, become, for an influential group of persons such as Sevso, a surprisingly comfortable place.[31]

The ancient collective representation of the *mundus* gave to such people – to Christians quite as much as to pagans – imaginative room for manœuvre. Its many layers reconciled faith in the One, High God with dogged, indeed reverential, concern for the things of the *saeculum*, that had once been ascribed, more frankly, to the care of the ancient gods. Whenever we meet groups involved in mobilising the 'set of symbolic forms' that expressed the unbroken will to rule of the Roman empire, in its major cities and most stable regions, we find ceremonials which, though not 'pagan' in the strict sense (in that blood-sacrifice was pointedly avoided), nevertheless aimed to sink the Roman order into the refulgent stability of the heavens, thereby making of the Roman *saeculum* on earth an image of that high region of the *mundus*, through which the magical energies of eternity pulsed with palpable splendour.[32]

We know how long such ceremonies survived in the Hippodrome and in the Imperial Palace of Constantinople, as the eastern empire settled down, after 395, to enjoy a *pax byzantina*, an east Roman peace as miraculously prolonged, in the eastern provinces, as any enjoyed in the Antonine age.[33] But it comes as a surprise to learn that, in the West, in the 440s, in an anxious age, overshadowed by the empire of Attila, the most Catholic princes of Ravenna would still take part in the great New Year's festival of the Kalends of January. On that occasion, the glory of the *saeculum* was made manifest in the procession that accompanied the nomination of the consuls of the year. The *tota officina idolorum*, the majestic décor of the ancient gods, was mobilised to relive a moment of cosmic euphoria. Men dressed as the mighty planets (in fact, as the gods of Rome) swirled solemnly through the Hippodrome of Ravenna, bringing to earth the promise of renewal, in yet another effulgence of the eternal energy of Rome.[34]

But we know of this occasion not, as we would in Byzantium, from a *Book of Ceremonies*, religiously preserved by the imperial court, but from the shocked comment of the then Catholic bishop of Ravenna, Petrus Chrysologus: *sacrilegio vetusto anni novitas consecratur*, 'The new birth of the year is blessed by outworn sacrilege.'[35] His remarks remind us that a new, sharp breeze had risen in the West. It had, indeed, blown for over a generation. For many Christians, such as Petrus Chrysologus, it seemed as if Christianisation, far from participating unproblematically in the euphoria of a world restored, associated with the Constantinian empire, had only just begun. It is to this change of mood that we must turn.

The change is as elusive in its onset, but as unmistakable, as a change of pitch in the hum of an engine. It is easier to describe than to explain. But I have been emboldened to linger upon it by a recent masterpiece of lucid and deeply pondered historical judgment, by Robert Markus' *The End of Ancient Christianity*.[36] What follows involves a working-through, from my own perspective, of one of his own most felicitous contentions – that a history of Christianisation in late antiquity and in the early middle ages must begin with close attention to what Christians themselves considered to be 'Christianisation'. It must involve entering into what constituted their own measure of success. It must respect the imaginative horizons within which late Roman Christians thought they could act. In the late fourth-century West, in the age of Ambrose and Augustine, these imaginative horizons shifted; and this change was exploited by an articulate and influential group of Christians.

In the first place, owing to the renewal of civil wars and the consequent weakening of crucial frontiers that followed the battle of Adrianople, in 378, the *saeculum* itself came to seem less secure. Put bluntly, Sevso's Pannonia, to take only one instance, became a far from happy place. The previous consensus that had been fostered by what I am tempted to call 'the first Christian empire' had depended on a shared prosperity that no longer existed.

This is a somewhat external and inevitably hypothetical consideration. What we do know is that, in many regions and strata of society, Christianity itself had changed. It is important to remember, in this respect, that the breakdown of religious prejudice does not always augur well for the cause of religious tolerance. Clear-cut enmities and firm codes of avoidance, based on a sharp sense of pollution, can have the effect of protecting religious

groups from each other. It gives them room to back off.
Constantine and his successors had been vehement in not wishing
to be seen near a sacrificial altar. They were expected to 'recoil
with horror from the blood of sacrifices'.[37] In Africa, the Donatist
church had based its claim to a monopoly of holiness on a similar
sense of revulsion: its founding fathers had avoided the stench
of altars at the time of the Great Persecution.[38] The avoidance of
pollution by pagan rites, and not the spread of the Gospel through
the total suppression of pagan worship, weighed most heavily with
the average Christian of the post-Constantinian age. In around
400, Publicola, a landowner with estates in Africa – possibly
Valerius Publicola, the son of Melania the elder – deluged
Augustine with a series of questions, all of which turned on issues
of pollution and avoidance, as these were faced on a day-to-day
basis by Christian peasants and estate-managers in a largely pagan
countryside. They concerned taking shares of crops blessed by
pagan rituals, eating fruit found beside pagan altars (that may have
been offered to the gods at the altar), washing in baths where
pagan statues stood and where the smell of incense lay heavy in the
air.[39] Augustine considered these questions fussy and misplaced.
Yet they reveal very clearly the horizons of the possible with which
average well-to-do Christians viewed their world. A strong sense
of pollution, focussed on the act of pagan sacrifice and its
associated rituals, was framed in such a way as to imply both that
paganism lay outside their own community and that it was there
to stay.

Such codes of avoidance were further validated by the highly
compartmentalised view of the *mundus* to which we have referred.
Given the rigid division between a High God and the lower
powers, it was not surprising that many persons should continue
to seek protection from the lower powers. Christians might claim
to know better: they would avoid 'the ceremonies of a by-gone

superstition' (to use the blunt words of Constantine).[40] But they retained a healthy respect for their efficacy. Leading members of Augustine's congregation at Hippo opined that rites performed for so long according to the ancient *libri pontificales* must have enjoyed the favour of God, and that it was only modern, secretive magic that should be condemned. Centuries later, Byzantines were convinced that whole cities had been protected from earthquakes by talismans, devised by wise philosophers, such as Apollonius of Tyana, who knew how to placate and hold at bay the uncanny forces of the lower air.[41]

Christians who thought like this did not feel polluted in the eyes of God that pagan rites continued to exist. It was sufficient that they themselves should remain clean. This attitude was summed up in the ruling of the pre-Constantinian Council of Elvira: landowners who feared the violence of their slaves would not be held guilty for having failed to forbid sacrifices on their estates; it was enough that they should not participate in them.[42] Apart from that, the compartmentalised nature of their universe gave many Christians every reason for doing very little about the beliefs and practices of their non-Christian neighbours.

On this topic, we may be confronted with a development as imperceptible as a generational change. Bishops, such as Ambrose of Milan, are usually treated as having been the decisive figures in late fourth-century Latin Christianity: they are held to have bullied the laity, from the emperor downwards, into a less tolerant mood. But the clergy may have sensed that the horizons of the possible had begun to change, also, for a new generation of powerful lay Christians. They could be expected to do more. Furthermore, some, at least, may have been anxious to do so: Christianity had become one of the symbolic forms through which they made their power more present to their inferiors.[43]

We know of this change of mood largely from the writing

and preaching of Christian clergymen who strove to communicate more exclusive attitudes to lay persons. Many such lay persons, of course, remained singularly hard of hearing when it came to suggestions that they upset long-established religious compromises. Yet we should not underestimate the long-term impact of a new, more drastic definition of monotheism on notions of authority among lay elites. In many provinces of the Western empire, in the course of the late fourth and fifth centuries, Christian exhortation presented the elites with a new model of power. It assumed a chain of command drawn as starkly on earth as it was in heaven. An emperor, hailed by Ambrose as *militans pro Deo*, on active service for the Christian God, was linked to his upper-class subjects, and, through these, to all inhabitants of the empire.

Such clarity of line was helped, also, by the language of asceticism. Wealth, culture and authority – the goals of the *saeculum* – were bleakly demystified and relativised in the language of the many ascetic Christians who wrote letters to the powerful. Yet, precisely because they were relativised, these social forces came to be validated, on condition that they were used, actively and for a clearly defined purpose. They were no longer unproblematic – immovable features of a society where power on earth was thought of as no more than a comforting reflection of the stability of the *mundus* above. Power over others, superiorities of wealth and culture, were not to be taken for granted. They were direct gifts from a High God. Their principal justification on earth was their active deployment in the service of His Church.

Service of the Church could extend to all places and situations. For an imperial administration and a landed aristocracy which now faced, in heightened form – at a time of political dislocation associated with the barbarian invasions – the perennial problem of how to make their presence felt at a distance, to ally with a more exclusive and universalist notion of monotheism was to gain a strong sense of agency on the local level. It was to believe that actions pleasing to God could be microcosmic re-enactments, in one's own region, of a universal order. The presence of a pagan temple, of an altar, of a schismatic conventicle on a faraway estate became, even for a relatively minor representative of the Roman order, an opportunity to show, in its destruction, paternal authority over others, rendered active and majestic by the service of the one God. Churches set up on estates, gifts to the local clergy, the support of local zealots in the destruction of shrines, such as that enjoyed by Saint Martin in Gaul from landowning families, ensured a more prominent role for Christian lay persons as *filii ecclesiae*, loyal and visible 'sons of the church' in their own city and region. These gestures brought a Christianised lay elite appreciably closer to the distant basis of their wealth at a time of growing uncertainty, when safety lay, in fact, in being on the spot, and active, no longer on an empire-wide scale, but within the narrow confines of one's province and one's local network of estates.

When we turn to Saint Augustine, and especially to the sermons that he preached in Carthage, between 397 and 404 AD (at a time of intense excitement, generated by the imperial decision to close the temples in the city and throughout Africa), we can see what this change of mood could mean to future generations. The significance of these sermons has been clearly pointed out by Robert Markus, in his *End of Ancient Christianity*. The tone of these years has now been further illuminated by a remarkable discovery. François Dolbeau has identified a whole series of long sermons by Augustine from this time, in a manuscript in the Public Library of Mainz, where they had lain for centuries, hidden from the gaze of classical philologists beneath the unprepossessing exterior of a crabbed, late Gothic hand.[44] Let me conclude, therefore, by lingering a little on the implications of Augustine's attitude, as this can be seen against the background that I have sketched out for previous generations.

Like Shenoute, his younger contemporary in Egypt, Augustine proposed to his congregation a passionate monotheism that cut through the lower layers of the *mundus*. *Salus tua ego sum* is the cry of the heart to a unique and ever-present God. *Si ad aeterna, quare non ad temporalia?* 'If relevant to eternity, why not to the present time?'[45] And, imperceptibly, all Carthage has become Augustine's church. For when Augustine rejected the Donatist claim that the holiness of the Church was based exclusively on avoidance of the pollution associated with essentially external, pagan rites, he burst the dam that held back the waters of a stern Catholic moralism from sweeping down upon the city as a whole. There was no part of its exuberant life that could claim to stand outside an all-engulfing Catholic church. This torrent would destroy not only identifiable pagan practices, such as the abhorrent rite of sacrifice. It threatened to drag in its wake, also, a sizeable area of the profane ceremonial life of Carthage. Carthage was a proud city. Its inhabitants, pagan and Christian alike, still expected to celebrate the security of the *saeculum* through ceremonies that linked city and *mundus* in the manner we have described, ceremonies performed, in this case, in honour of the statue of the *genius* of Carthage – a majestic figure, carrying the abundant fruits of Africa in her arms, as befitted the capital of the breadbasket of Rome.[46]

Augustine would no longer allow this. Behaviour deemed inappropriate in a Christian came to include far more than participating in pagan rites, around the smoking altars. The songs, dances and banquets associated with civic life were condemned. Their solemn, public character was denied. Their diffuse religiosity was bleakly demystified. Public ceremonies were caricatured by being spoken of, exclusively, in moral terms, as if they were no more than occasions for debauchery.[47] New codes of Christian decorum were proposed. Even terms of speech, such as the continued use of the names of the gods for the days of the week, were deemed unsuitable. It was better to pick up the habit of the *ecclesiasticus ritus*, of a Catholic usage, that spoke of *prima feria, secunda feria*:[48] by which high standards only Portugal, among Western Catholic nations, should be considered fully Christianised!

The wayward soul could sacrifice to the demonic powers in innumerable ways, without ever approaching a pagan altar. At a time when the city outside the Catholic basilica hummed with the annual euphoria of the feast of the Kalends of January, in 404, Augustine preached a sermon of two and a quarter hours (the longest he ever preached at Carthage). The list of civic enjoyments that he condemned covered celebrations that had been judged innocent by Christians of an earlier generation. He ends his enumeration with a crushing *quasi*: those who do these things act *as if* 'they offered incense to the demons, taken from their very own hearts'.[49]

In these years, Augustine, the sombre theorist of the force of habit in human affairs, added a final touch of shade to what has become the modern, Western representation of Christianisation. At the same time as he spoke for his colleagues, the bishops of Africa, in urging an ambitious programme, Augustine offered them what they needed to maintain such an enterprise – he provided a cogent explanation in the event of failure.

In so doing, Augustine contributed decisively to the notion of Christianisation with which we ourselves still live. In the early fifth century, Christian critics brought to the fore a 'representation' of their own times, that was the dark counterpoint to the triumphant narrative that circulated in other circles – the narrative of supernatural victory over the gods with which we began this chapter. A myth of the 'decline of the Church' began to circulate, especially in Latin ascetic circles. The notion, of course, had always lain to hand, and was used by Christian preachers, such as Origen and Chrysostom, in order to rebuke their congregations for having degenerated from the high standards of an earlier age. But the notion of the 'decline of the Church' became, now, a major explanatory device for the entire present state of Christianity. The Church was no longer undermined by the demons, through heresy. Decline had taken place for more prosaic, but more insuperable, reasons. Success had 'cooled' the zeal of the original Christian communities.[50] Even Christian worship itself had come to be tainted by the sheer weight of new adherents. In effect, any practice of which a group of self-styled *districtiores christiani*, of 'more rigorous Christians',[51] happened to disapprove was now confidently ascribed to habits brought into the Church by recent converts from paganism. The Church may have defeated the gods; but it had not defeated, in its own congregations, the towering force of religious habits taken directly from the non-Christian past.

In 392, Augustine was faced, as a priest at Hippo, by a delegation of old-style Catholics, who regarded their exuberant funerary customs and their association of feasting with the celebration of the cult of the martyrs – with good reason – as wholly Christian traditions, to which they had been accustomed for generations. He gave them a historical explanation of the situation in which they found themselves. After the conversion of Constantine, he said, 'crowds of the heathen' had wished to enter the Church. They could not bear to give up the 'revelling and drunkenness with which they had been accustomed to celebrate the feasts of the idols'.[52] A soft-hearted (or opportunistic) clergy had let them in. Hence the practice. Hence Augustine's decision to abolish it.

From that time onwards, such a view tends to be taken for granted, as a common-sense glimpse of the obvious. Untouched, today, by the sense of tragedy that stirred those who first propounded it, we tend to agree with Augustine's diagnosis. Yet what was at stake was less clear-cut than Augustine made it appear to be. It was largely an issue of authority. Augustine and his clerical colleagues claimed to be able to tell the Christian laity exactly what paganism had been and how much of it survived in their own religious practices within the Church.

This claim involved nothing less than a subtle 'historicisation', even a 'laicisation', of paganism. The end of paganism was caught in normal time – it was mired in the slow and erratic processes observed, by Augustine and similar moralists, in the healing of any other bad habit. The idea of the supernatural triumph of Christ over the kingdom of the demons remained; but it was joined by another theme. For pagan worship itself was not an exclusively supernatural matter. The power of the demons was less clearly focussed. It showed itself not only in sacrifice, but also in centuries of misdirected habit, that had affected all aspects of ancient life. While pagan worship might be abolished, the past remained a pagan place. Those who entered the Church brought with them the shadow of an untranscended, ancient way of life. *Antiquitas*, 'antiquity, mother of all evils', was the last enemy of all true Christians.[53]

Within such a perspective, the Christian believer was no longer presented, in largely supernatural terms, as poised between sin and salvation, between the pollution of idols and an instant freedom from the demonic, brought about by the vibrant power of Christ. The believer was poised, also, between two cultures, even between two historical epochs – between the growing Christian culture of the Catholic Church, with its own theology and its own distinctive habits of speech and worship, and a profane world whose roots reached back in time into the rich soil of a past once ruled by the *dei buggiardi*. It was a past whose darkened majesty would be conjured up with memorable circumstantiality, for all future Latin readers, in the pages of Augustine's *City of God.*

These views were not only stated by Augustine. They characterised a generation of mainly Latin writers. But they were by no means universal. The Christian historians who propounded the 'representation' of the fourth century with which we began this chapter looked back, rather, to a historiographical tradition largely associated with Eusebius of Caesarea – to a very different version of the history of the human race from that proposed by Augustine. Greek writers of the fifth century AD, such as the historian and apologist Theodoret of Cyrrhus, lingered, by preference, on the excitements of a great *metabolé*.[54] They chose to celebrate a mighty transmutation, by which the non-Christian past flowed into a triumphant Christian present. It amounted to a declaration of total victory, that left much of the past untouched. The Roman past brought no troubling associations into the present. Even the statues of Livia and Augustus outside the Prytaneion of Ephesus would continue to stand throughout this period. With the sign of the cross neatly carved on their foreheads, they gazed down serenely on the prelates assembled by the emperor Augustus' orthodox successor, Theodosius II, to the great Council of 431.[55]

Yet, in the Western parts of the empire, the basic narrative of Christianisation, with which we moderns are most familiar, had been created. It is some indication of the distance between ourselves and late Roman persons that this particular narrative was not the one that counted for most at that time. One suspects that Christianisation still meant, for the majority of fourth- and fifth-century Christians, the story of a stunning, supernatural victory over their gods. The alternative story, offered by the critics of their own age, however, lends itself more readily to a historian's saddened sense of the possible. We take for granted that Christianisation must have been a slow, heroic struggle on earth against the unyielding, protean weight of an unconverted ancient world. Thanks largely to the writings of the generation of Augustine, a charged memory of the Roman past now lingers in the imagination of all Westerners as a potent fragment of 'encapsulated history'. *Antiquitas*, an ancient, pagan past that dogged the Christian present, lay close to the heart of medieval Christendom – an inescapable, endlessly fascinating companion, tinged with sadness and with a delicious sense of danger, a synecdoche of human nature itself, lived out under the shadow of Adam's sin. It is for this reason that the Christianisation of the Roman world has remained a problem. The scholar must still struggle hard to catch a glimpse, behind the reassuring familiarity of a story told continuously in Western Europe from the fifth century onwards, of the outlines of a world profoundly unlike our own, in which the decisive changes of this period took place.

Chapter 2

THE LIMITS OF INTOLERANCE

✛

I HAVE BEEN PROMPTED TO RE-THINK THE PROBLEM OF intolerance in the later empire by the experience of my nephew when, at the age of three, he paid his first visit to the Cincinnati Zoo. He already knew what all the animals looked like. He had seen pictures of elephants, giraffes, lions and walruses. But the only living animal that he had actually seen was his own pet cat, Teddy. Naturally, he assumed, therefore, that all animals were the same size as that cat – and, consequently, that they were smaller than himself: a flattering assumption. The fact that the animals in the zoo were all of very different sizes – some, indeed, immeasurably larger than himself – came as a great surprise to him. On seeing two Bengal tigers eating their lunch, he exclaimed: 'Big, BIG cats!', and remained silent, *adtonitus*, for a full twenty minutes, until a visit to the bird-house restored his over-shadowed ego.

Religious intolerance is a phenomenon that bulks large in any history of late antiquity, to such an extent that it colours our perception of the entire quality of the age. The historian who wishes to form a just estimate of its nature, extent and effects has to face the same puzzlement as did this young fellow. We are dealing with a phenomenon that is documented in vivid, and seemingly unambiguous, fragments of evidence. The problem is, how to assess the relative *size* of the phenomena to which the fragments allude. How does the well-known intolerance of the post-Constantinian empire fit into our general picture of late Roman society as a whole and of its workings? Is it the size of a cat, or did it loom, at the time, as vast as an elephant? Above all, what other beasts were around, to provide us with a scale with which to measure its relative bulk in the minds and actions of contemporaries?

One thing is certain: the notion of toleration, at that time, is not to be found among the elephants. In his introduction to the 1983 Conference of the Ecclesiastical History Society, devoted to the theme of *Persecution and Toleration*, Sir Geoffrey Elton could afford to be blunt:

> religions organised in powerful churches and in command of the field persecute as a matter of course and tend to regard toleration as a sign of weakness or even of wickedness towards whatever deity they worship. Among the religious, toleration is demanded by the persecuted who need it if they are to become triumphant, when, all too often, they start to persecute in their turn. A highly unsubtle interplay of persecution and toleration thus conveniently sums up the millennia of religious history and more especially of ecclesiastical history. To say this is not cynicism, but sobriety of judgement.[1]

His bleak view was confirmed by Peter Garnsey in the first article in the collection, devoted to 'Religious Toleration in Classical Antiquity'.[2] If, by toleration, we mean an active concept – that is, 'disapproval or disagreement coupled with an unwillingness to take action against those who are viewed with disfavour in the interest of some moral or political principle', we will not find it in this period. He went on to point out that 'the contrast commonly drawn for the world of classical antiquity between a tolerant paganism and an intolerant Christianity'[3] was based upon a misapprehension of Greek and Roman religion. In Athens '[t]he citizen was not so much encouraged to exert his individuality as reminded of his duty to abide by the laws and customs of the community'.[4] In the vastly more complex society of imperial Rome, 'the one sure maxim of extended empire, a wise and salutary neglect' seems to have held sway: 'it is permissible to attribute to Rome's leaders nothing more grandiose than an appreciation of the distinctness of the different peoples who made up their empire, combined with an implicit recognition of their inability to control their subjects beyond a certain point and the unwisdom of rousing local passions'.[5] As for Christianity, apart from the brilliant pleading of Tertullian '[t]he Christian contribution to toleration theory peters out with the cessation of persecution and the upturn of the Church's fortunes'.[6]

Garnsey's austere delineation of the limits of toleration in the ancient world has been confirmed by the recent article of François Paschoud, in the collection devoted to *L'intolleranza cristiana nei confronti dei pagani*, published in *Cristianesimo nella Storia* for 1990. With his habitual clarity, Paschoud sums up the situation for fourth-century pagans. They were as inflexible in their expectations as were the Christians.[7] We are dealing with two groups condemned to total incomprehension: *un décevant dialogue des sourds*; 'les païens ne pouvant concevoir les rites traditionnels que dans un cadre officiel, célébrés par le monarque et les dignitaires civils aux frais de l'Etat'. From Constantine onwards, such a situation became impossible for a Christian head of state. It was only a matter of time before the end came. 'Ce durcissement était logique, prévisible, inévitable; le chrétien a le devoir d'annoncer la bonne nouvelle, le prosélytisme est pour lui une obligation.'[8] Seen from this perspective, the fourth century is frozen. It is by no means a 'Wavering Century'. It is no more than a tense lull, waiting for the bomb to drop. Ambrose and Theodosius I finally do what Constantine had made quite possible, by his conversion, in 312, and what Firmicus Maternus had already urged Constantine's successors to do, in 345. It is an entirely logical view of events; it lends itself to a crisp narrative, sign-posted with well-known dates, trenchant laws and familiar *dramatis personae*, whose sentiments, usually of spine-chilling clarity, when it came to the need for official intolerance, have survived in abundant written evidence. It is not necessarily good history. It certainly does not capture the horizons of the possible of known pagan authors, such as Ammianus Marcellinus and the quirky author of the *Scriptores Historiae Augustae*, nor even of a Christian preacher, in a major city, such as John Chrysostom.[9] Such fourth-century persons did not have the benefit of Professor Paschoud's article to spell out for them the writing on the wall for a whole, non-Christian way of life and worship.

Paschoud's perspective reflects, in fact, an influential, but idiosyncratic, pagan refraction of the Christian ecclesiastical narrative to which I drew attention in the previous chapter. As we have seen, Christian historians of the early fifth century had tended to represent the establishment of the Christian empire as a brisk undertaking, long prepared in heaven. Constantine had begun to close down pagan worship. The delay caused by the rise of the Arian heresy within the church, and the chill, passing cloud of the three-year reign of Julian the Apostate, ensured that the predestined collapse of paganism had to wait until the reign of Theodosius I. 'The worship of idols, which on the initiative of Constantine had begun to sink into neglect and to be subjected to destruction, fell completely when Theodosius was emperor.'[10]

We should remember that a major source for Paschoud's view of the fourth century was the *New History* of the pagan count

Zosimus. This was a reworking, in the early sixth century, of the *History* of Eunapius of Sardis of 404. Zosimus simply inverted the triumphant Christian narrative. In his account, also, the imperial initiative was decisive. Already, for Eunapius, and certainly for Zosimus, absolute, single rule, instituted with the foundation of the Roman empire, was a *damnosa haereditas*, which, sooner or later, was bound to place the venerable religious establishment of Rome in the hands of impious and negligent tyrants. Constantine abandoned the rites; Theodosius I refused to allow state funds for their performance in the name of the empire; no longer supported by sacrifices performed on its behalf, the Western empire fell. It was all as simple as that.[11]

It was easy to think such thoughts, alternately euphoric or bleak, but always appropriately emperor-centred, in a world capital such as fifth-century Constantinople. Even the legal commission which assembled the *Theodosian Code*, in 436–8, made their own, implicit but long-lasting contribution to the official, Christian narrative of the fourth century. As in all other books of the *Code*, the imperial laws on heretics, Jews and pagans, collected in the sixteenth book, were arranged in chronological order, starting with the emperor Constantine. Through this fact alone, they presented the legislation of the age in rising strains, that reached a crescendo in the reign of Theodosius II. All laws were seen to have led up to the new Christian dispensation, where, in the words of the second *Novella* of Theodosius, 'a thousand terrors of the laws' had been set in place, to uphold the *insatiabilis honor*, 'the boundless claim to honour' of the Catholic Church.[12] What is at stake is the 'pace' of the fourth century and, so, the expectations of the Jews and pagans who lived through it.

Yet, however much a retrospective certainty, shared alike by disillusioned pagans and by triumphant Christians, may have distorted our impression of these expectations, the basic point made by Garnsey and Paschoud remains valid – in strict theory, at least, intolerance held the day.

Yet, before we hustle the notion of toleration off to the Small Animal House, we should look at it more carefully. It was not an effective notion in restraining the actions of the powerful; but this was not simply because, being both religiously minded and of autocratic temper, authoritative figures, such as emperors and bishops, were bound to be bigots. The notion itself rested on a very slender basis. Both cognitively and socially it was confined to a narrow niche in the intellectual ecology of the classical world. It bore the clear stamp of the philosophical circles in which it had originated, and beyond which it rarely ventured.

Throughout the late classical period, philosophers were at one and the same time admired and mocked by their contemporaries for practising a form of hyper-individualism. Though often a man of high status and culture, the philosopher presented himself as a person pointedly free from power. He had rejected office, in his city and at court, and the accumulation of wealth that invariably went with the opportunities for self-enrichment associated with the exercise of power. He did this with the same, instinctive horror as he frequently rejected heavy, red meat; and with considerably more horror than he rejected the embraces of his wife. Power, not sex, was what was held to have polluted him.[13] The philosopher lived by his free *logos* alone. He did not feel bound, as the majority of unthinking persons of his own class felt themselves to be bound, by the heavy restraints of *nomos* – by respect for traditional custom and for the obligation imposed by traditional civic ritual. If a philosopher made religious choices, he was expected to justify and to communicate these without peremptory commands and without slavish appeals to common custom. When the philosopher Porphyry learned that his friend, Firmus Castricius, had abandoned the vegetarian life, he wrote 'that it appeared to me that it would be too rustic and remote from the rational method of persuasion to reprehend you'. Only unphilosophical persons, such as Jews and Syro-Phoenicians, considered it heroic to maintain flood taboos, as a matter of ancestral custom, without justifying them by reasoned argument.[14]

Above all, the philosopher's model of relations with the divine world was a model pared down to the barest essentials of intimate, because totally free, human relations. We see this most clearly in philosophical attitudes to 'superstition'. Superstition did not mean what it means to modern persons. Outside Epicurean circles, superstition was not treated as a cognitive aberration – an 'irrational' belief in nonexistent or misperceived beings. Superstition was a social *gaffe* committed in the presence of the gods. It betrayed a lack of the ease and candour that were supposed to characterise a free man's relations with any persons, human or divine. Excessive observance was strictly analogous to flattery and ostentation; and magic was a form of graft and manipulation. Forced belief, therefore, was subsumed beneath the same, disapproving, rubric. It was treated as the exact equivalent of the love which a tyrant sought, in vain, to extort, through fear, from servile courtiers.[15]

This was a heroic model of religious conduct. But it was a somewhat etiolated one. Stressing as it did an uncompromising authenticity in person-to-person relations, it deliberately looked through the heavier social and intellectual reasons for consent to religious beliefs, that played an important role in the life and imagination of most ancient persons – that is, respect for the weight of tradition and for the binding force of civic loyalties. Not even philosophers maintained such an extreme stance on all occasions. When faced by the impiety of the Christians, both Celsus and Porphyry emerged as fierce defenders of *nomos*, of traditional religious custom, enforced, if needs be, by punishment: they wasted no tears on Christian martyrs.[16]

Philosophers did, at least, add one important cognitive dimension to their position. Just as, for Heraclitus, nature wished to test the mind by hiding herself from the unperceptive observer, so a distant God might be believed to wish to inspire even greater awe and yearning, through playing hide and seek with His worshippers. It is the argument adduced by the philosopher Themistius, in his fifth *Oration*, for the emperor Jovian, in 363, and in a speech delivered before the emperor Valens, in 377, reported by Sozomen in his *Ecclesiastical History*. He is said to have advised Valens

> that he ought not to wonder at the dissension concerning ecclesiastical doctrines, for it was more moderate and less than among the pagans . . . [Indeed] it might probably be pleasing to God not to be so easily known, and to have a divergence of opinion, so that each might fear Him the rather, since an accurate knowledge of Him is so unattainable. And in the very attempt to summarise this vastness, one would tend to conclude how great He is and how good He is.[17]

The fact that truth was valued more, and that its transcendent quality was frequently appreciated all the more intensely if acquired with difficulty, was a fixed component in the thought both of pagan Platonists and of Christian theologians, such as Gregory Nazianzen.[18] The psychology of longing aroused by the allegorical method rested on similar foundations. And if the gaining of truth took time, and might even include periods of doubt, then a certain interim margin of error must be allowed to the seeker.

Yet one only had to look at a professional philosopher such as Themistius to know that he was not for real. Themistius was a past-master at the art of ostentatiously rejecting the marks of power. When dining with the emperors, he was always careful to wear his philosopher's dark *tribônion*. He even eschewed an official salary.[19] But it was impossible not to notice that Themistius usually made his appearance when the emperor was intending to back down from a course of action that had proved unfeasible or unpopular. To read Themistius on Goths (as this has now been convincingly explained by Peter Heather's *Goths and Romans*) is the best way we have to understand Themistius on religious toleration. On that occasion, he had been given a difficult assignment: he had to find the elevating tones that enabled the emperor Valens to admit that he had failed. In a tense interview in the broiling sun on a barge in the middle of the Danube, in 369, the Gothic king, Athanaric, had indicated in no uncertain terms to Valens that he and his tribe would not be pushed around. The projected imperial expedition into Gothia was quietly cancelled; and Themistius found himself waxing eloquent on the benefits of defence-cuts and of multicultural-ism.[20] In much the same way, Themistius spoke of toleration, in 363, in his fifth *Oration*, at a time of deep uncertainty and potential vindictiveness, after the death of Julian, and again, in 377, when Valens' alliance with the Homoian party had begun to run out of steam.[21] On both occasions, the context of Themistius' speech effectively cancelled out its content. Such speeches were not resonant statements of principle. They were usually no more than making the best of a bad job. They were discreet, but unmistakable, signals of failure. Admirable though such senti-ments might be, they were not invariably welcome in an empire that valued momentum and that genuinely feared infirmity of purpose in high places.

The philosopher moved in a basically conformist upper-class world. I do not mean conformist only in the pejorative sense.

In the Roman empire, young men of the upper classes were socialised, from childhood up, to reverence ancestral custom, to value solidarity, and to appreciate and use power. To his peers, the philosopher was an invaluable safety-valve. He was a licensed maverick in an otherwise deadly serious class of persons. But his views were scarcely relevant to their own position. If members of the governing class set limits to intolerance, they did so by drawing on very different traditions from those associated with the philosopher.

I would suggest that, in seeking to define notions of tolerance and intolerance in late antiquity in largely intellectual terms, we have been misled by a modern predilection. We have placed undue emphasis on statements by philosophers and by Christian apologists, who styled themselves as philosophers. Theory will not get us very far in the later empire. It is too fragile a pick-lock to turn the heavy tumblers of the mentality of a fundamentally authoritarian, yet complex, governing class. For the rest of this chapter, I would like, rather, to draw attention to some less articulate, but decisive, factors connected with the day-to-day practice of the later empire. It is these mute restraints, and not the deceptively clear statements of theorists on either side, that cut the vast notional intolerance of the post-Constantinian empire down to size.

I would like to suggest, inevitably very briefly, that the surprising number of fragments of evidence for the peaceful coexistence of persons of different faiths throughout the late Roman period, and for persistent short-fall in the application of intolerant laws, make sense if seen in terms of long-established techniques of government that were embedded in traditional codes of behaviour. It is not simply a matter of pointing to the unavoidable hiatus between theory and practice, brought about by the merciful, systemic incompetence of the imperial administration in enforcing its own laws. What mattered more than administrative inertia was the retarding effect, in an age of religious change, of attitudes and ways of getting things done that came from a pre-Christian past, and were observed to have remained effective in the late Roman present. It is the 'viscosity' of the mentality of the elites of the later empire that deserves to be emphasised. This viscosity ensured that the new, peremptory statements of intolerance, which bulk so large in our written sources, do not quite fit what can be known, in considerable detail, of the rest of late Roman society. One is reminded of those late reworkings of classical portraits that can be seen in many museums. The drastic tidying of the hair, the rounding of the eyes, the smoothing of the cheeks into an expression of hieratic austerity cannot quite disguise the unmistakable 'set' of a Julio-Claudian jaw. It is to this 'set of the jaw' of the late Roman elites, a 'set' based on a very ancient practice of politics as the art of the possible in an imperial system, that we should turn.

There is one feature of the practice of politics that is directly relevant to the impact of religious intolerance in this period. For all its autocratic overtones, and horrendous reputation in most modern accounts of the age, it is well known that the imperial government continued to depend, to a very large extent, for its effectiveness, on the consensus of a widely diffused network of local elites. *Devotio*, the loyalty and prompt obedience that was expected of upper-class subjects of the empire, had to be wooed, or, at least, not allowed to go entirely off the boil – it could not be imposed by force alone. In this process of mobilising loyalty, we should not underestimate the importance of appeals to shared codes of behaviour. Our most explicit evidence for the creation and functioning of these codes comes from the highly governed Greek provinces of the empire; but the phenomenon was empire-wide. *Paideia*, the careful grooming of young males according to a traditional canon of decorum and of literary excellence, was held to have the effect of socialising rulers and ruled alike. *Devotio*, therefore, was both offered and demanded according to an ancient ideal of civility. As a result, the exercise of power in a hard-driving and potentially abrasive system was not controlled, in the sense of being subject to legal restraints. But it had to be, at least, rendered dignified. Power might be all too real and intrusive; but it needed to be naturalised, by acquiring an aura of ceremonious majesty. Like a miraculous calm spreading across the face of a choppy ocean, the 'serenity' associated with the vast notional omnipotence of the emperor was mediated, throughout the imperial system, by a succession of representatives and collaborators, by means of innumerable interchanges in which courtesy, self-control and quiet confidence – the marks of innate superiority – were believed to have prevailed. As a result, among the elites, the issue of toleration was swallowed up in a specifically late Roman emphasis on civility. *Paideia*, not philosophy, set the limits to intolerance.

We are dealing with an upper class which accepted that authority, fear, the direct use of force against religious places and even, if less frequently, against religious enemies, should be mobilised to impose truth and to banish error. Yet precisely because it was expected that authority would be used in matters of religion, the manner in which this authority was asserted was subjected to sharp and anxious scrutiny. Correct religion was held to be the glory of the empire; and precisely for this reason, the manner in which uniformity was imposed had to reflect all the more faithfully the overbearing dignity of the imperial power. It carried with it strong overtones of serenity and persuasive force. For these qualities were the hallmark of power, and of the authority of those who represented it in their locality. A society which, to a modern observer, appears to have carried dangerously few theoretical antibodies to intolerance was nonetheless capable of registering, with considerable sensitivity, those moments when the imposition of religious conformity, or the settling of religious grievances, took place in a manner or at a pace that did not mesh with long-established, implicit codes of public behaviour. When it came to the limits of religious intolerance in the later empire, we can apply the words of Paul Veyne (when speaking of a different matter): '[t]he . . . options of antiquity did not lie where we should look for them . . . but where we should *not* look for them . . . in the mode of obedience, the style of command'.[22]

We can appreciate this preoccupation with a 'style of command' on many levels. For all the development of a centralised bureaucracy, that bulks so large in late Roman sources, the later empire still depended – to a quite surreal degree, in comparison with modern notions of the state – on the collaboration of local elites and on administrative structures based on the individual city, for the collection and the redistribution of its taxes.[23] This fact alone puts the religious passions of the time in perspective. Seen from the point of view of the civic notables of the fourth and fifth centuries, the annual paroxysm of the collection of taxes, which occurred in the territory of every city, and not religious affairs – however exciting these might be, and apparently urgent, to those who knew about such things, on a supernatural level – was the true elephant in the zoo of late Roman politics. It dwarfed all other occasions for the exercise and implementation of the emperor's will.

It is easy to assume that a tax-system so relentless – and apparently so successful – was no more than the thin end of the wedge, that it indicated the indomitable will of the emperors to control the souls of their subjects as surely as they had come to control their wealth. In fact, the exact opposite may be the case. In most areas, the system of negotiated consensus was usually stretched to its limits by the task of extracting taxes. It had little energy left over to give 'bite' to intolerant policies in matters of religion. It is not surprising that many late Roman sources take for granted that there was a clear relation between toleration and tax-yield. Faced by the demands of Porphyry of Gaza for permission to destroy the temples of the city, supposedly in 400, the emperor Arcadius is presented as having said: 'I know that the city is full of idols, but it shows *devotio* (*eugnômonei*) in paying its taxes, and contributes much to the treasury. It we suddenly terrorise these people, they will run away and we will lose considerable revenues.'[24] In the same way, the Praetorian Prefect, Taurus, was held to have intervened, in 432–3, to quash an edict that would have forced an unwelcome theological formula on the bishops of Cilicia: 'Entering into the imperial presence, he swore that the cities would be ruined, and stated quite plainly, that what Thrace [a province devastated by Hunnish raids] is now, Cilicia would be, where hardly a city remains to pay its taxes.'[25] Of both stories one should say *se non è vero ben trovato*: for even if imagined on each of these particular occasions, it was assumed that such arguments would carry weight with the emperor. They make one wonder how much the continued solvency of the eastern empire owed to innumerable, unspoken acts of *dissimulatio*, of turning a blind eye to local communities, who may have been all the more punctual in paying their taxes, if they needed to preserve from official inter-ference their ancestral religious practices.

There were good reasons why this should be so. In truly serious matters, such as the collection of taxes, it was already difficult to strike the right balance between browbeating and cajoling the local elites, without this delicate equilibrium, set in place every year, being upset by the righteous anger of the true believer. The need for a measure of courtesy in extorting conformity, and not any abstract idea of religious toleration, was a strategy that any late

Roman governor was expected to understand. It was with this in mind that Libanius approached the governor of Syria, Alexander of Baalbek, a vehement pagan, and a man with a reputation for bad temper and high-handedness, who had been appointed by Julian the Apostate, in part so as to harass Christians. Alexander had to deal with a recalcitrant Christian town-councillor of Apamea, on whose behalf Libanius intervened. Libanius reminded Alexander that although he was commendably zealous for the gods, _he must learn to play the game by the rules: 'Consider this . . . whether it is better to show gentleness and get the job done, or to show yourself a hard man and make matters hard for yourself.'[26]

Such letters, written by a pagan to protect Christians from the pagan representatives of Julian the Apostate, have been justly appreciated by modern scholars. They appear as 'an oasis of humane tolerance' in an age of violence.[27] But they are a tribute less to the prevalence of any notion of toleration than to the stability of an unassuming deposit of political good sense, which a master of _paideia_, such as Libanius, hoped to instil in the minds of all members of the upper class.

Nor were the restraints imposed by the concern for a specific 'style of command' limited only to the upper classes of provincial society. Power had to be naturalised on many levels. This is shown clearly by a letter, which has long languished unobserved in the appendix to the works of Sulpicius Severus, and which has now been edited and commented on by Claude Lepelley in _Antiquités Africaines_ for 1989. It takes us to an estate in North Africa.[28] It is a flattering note written by a smalltown notable, congratulating the local Catholic bishop on the successful coercion of a group of Donatist peasants.

One does not often have the good fortune to uncover so egregious, because so studiously disingenuous, a statement of the late Roman ideal of a mild and persuasive, because unchallenged, exercise of authority by the 'natural' leaders of society. Our writer is effusive. One might expect consent from the elite (many of whom had doubtless been Donatists): *Est enim prudentibus viris cum devotione cognatio*; 'There is a natural affinity between educated men and true religion.' But peasants were less promising material: *nec cito conveniens credulitati rusticitas*; 'While true belief is not immediately within the range of rustic minds'. They were hard stone to carve. Yet our bishop had done it – and without violence: *nullis minis, nullis omnino terroribus.*[29]

What we should note is that, after 411, threats and terror were the official order of the day. The law of 30 January 412 made this plain. Donatist *coloni* were equated to slaves; if recalcitrant, both were to undergo 'admonition' from their masters, in the form of the *verberum crebrior ictus*, a thorough flogging.[30] Yet, in many parts of Africa, *coloni* were considerably less passive than the rhetoric of the laws would give us to suppose. The *coloni* of an estate that had the misfortune to fall under the jurisdiction of a tyrannical Catholic bishop, Antoninus of Fussala, in the hinterland of Hippo Regius, simply told their landowner that they would leave the estate if they were not assigned to another diocese.[31] There was, therefore, a strong element of political good sense in the studiously mild approach affected by our bishop. His hands were tied by a social system that was already subject to strains more potentially murderous than those provoked by religious dissidence, and which he had no wish to upset by misplaced acts of brutality.

The letter gives us an unexpected glimpse of the late Roman social system at work in religious matters. For modern persons, it is not an altogether pleasant glimpse. If authority was to work without overt violence, it had to seem 'natural'; it had to relay commands with quiet certainty from a position of unchallenged superiority to persons whose inferiority, also, was to be taken for granted. As a result of the religious changes of the age, the social hierarchy became even more high pitched. Peasants, and increasingly *pagani*, pagans treated as no better than countryfolk, were consistently presented as passive and congenitally simple minded, so that they could be expected to follow the gentle, because orderly, lead of their natural superiors into the true faith. Among the upper classes, a combination of browbeating and cajolery was the stuff of late Roman politics. Such styles were transferred, without a moment's hesitation, to the new governmental effort to achieve religious conformity. A recurrent *obbligato* of ceremonious bullying, and not the occasional outburst of bigotry and outright religious violence, was by far the most obtrusive – and, to a modern reader, the most distasteful – feature of the religious politics of the age.

Yet, combined with an educational system that continued to emphasise decorum, poise and ceremonious good nature as the only appropriate public language of 'naturally' superior persons, the emphasis on the correct manner in which authority was to be asserted gave contemporaries, at least, some means of recognising an outright bully when they saw one. Here the ecclesiastical historians of fifth-century Constantinople are invaluable sources, most particularly the historian Socrates. A layman, a lawyer, himself a member of the minority community of the Novatians, Socrates had developed a sharp eye for such persons. But we must remember that it is a 'period eye' – an unmistakably late Roman eye, that does not ask, first, whether a powerful bishop is intolerant, but, rather, whether or not he will set about being intolerant in an acceptable manner.

The portrait of Nestorius, in the *Ecclesiastical History* of Socrates, is a memorable vignette of a 'hard' man. It could have been written by Ammianus Marcellinus, that master of the sinister physiognomics of power.[32] 'What sort of a disposition he was . . . those who possessed any discernment were able to perceive from his first sermon.' Newly ordained as the bishop of Constantinople, Nestorius mounted the *ambo* of Hagia Sophia and turned to the emperor: 'Give me, my prince, the earth purged of heretics, and I will give you heaven as a recompense.' This was far worse than intolerance. It was a lapse in good taste. The *cognoscenti* in the audience, 'who were skilful in predicating a man's character from his expressions did not fail to detect his levity of mind, and violent and vainglorious temperament, inasmuch as he had burst forth into such vehemence without being able to contain himself'.[33]

Included in the *Historia Tripartita* of Cassiodorus, passages such as this enjoyed an unexpected afterlife in Western Europe. They re-emerged, in the Reformation, first with Johann Brenz and, a little later, in Sebastian Castellio's *Concerning Heresies*, as prize exhibits in the sixteenth-century debate over the imposition of the death penalty on dissenters. It proved, to the liberal Reformers, that there were already many 'bloodthirsty bishops' around, in the reign of Theodosius II, prepared to lead this otherwise benign predecessor of the Holy Roman Emperor, Charles V, 'like a bull by the nose'.[34] In this manner, the opening of the modern debate on religious tolerance was fuelled by a characteristically late Roman portrayal of a breach in decorum.

We should never underestimate the silent pressure of the codes that weighed so heavily and so insistently on the members of late Roman elites. If we do so, it is because we often forget that the religious revolution associated with the conversion of Constantine was only one half of the story of the fourth-century empire. The other half, as we saw in passing in the previous chapter, was the formation of a new governing class, determined to enjoy the privileges of a world restored to order after generations of political uncertainty and humiliation for the *res Romana*. We are dealing with a society led by men in the grip of a 'lifeboat mentality'. Dramatic religious changes might be believed, by some, and especially by the Christian beneficiaries of the conversion of Constantine, to have helped to restore this order; but they were not to be allowed to rock the boat.

As far as the formation of the new governing class of the post-Constantinian empire was concerned, the fourth century was very definitely not a century overshadowed by 'The Conflict of Paganism and Christianity'. Nothing, indeed, would have been more distressing to a member of the late Roman upper classes than the suggestion that 'pagan' and 'Christian' were designations of overriding importance in their style of life and in their choice of friends and allies. Divisiveness in matters of religion, though relished by tidy-minded modern scholars, would have been a recipe for disaster. Rather, as we saw in the previous chapter, studied ambiguity and strong loyalty to common 'symbolic forms', which spoke with a strong, but religiously neutral, voice of the authority of the empire and the security of its social order, prevailed at this time.

If we want to find a particularly vivid example of the manner in which members of the elite shared common 'symbolic forms' despite their known religious differences, we need only turn to the correspondence of Libanius with the Jewish Patriarch, Gamaliel, of the house of Hillel, established in Palestine. It would be wrong to imply, as Menachem Stern has done, that the two men were drawn together 'by fellow feeling in the common plight in which Jews and "Hellenes" found themselves under the yoke of Christian emperors'.[35] They were drawn together by common enjoyment of an imperial system that conferred high status upon them both. The more we study the legal position of the Jewish Patriarch in the later Roman empire, the more we realise that it owed little or nothing to the continuous preservation of the notion of a Jewish state, represented by a Jewish leader, from the time of the suppression of the kingdom of Judaea. It was largely a creation of the post-Constantinian empire, even, perhaps, of the reign of Theodosius I.[36] Pagan *rhetor* and Jewish *nasi'* alike knew that they were at the top of the heap, for the time being at least, by the good graces of a Christian court that could not afford to dispense with their services. Both enjoyed high honorary rank, conferred on them by imperial *codicilli* – those precious purple letters of personal esteem signed by Theodosius in his own hand.

Not surprisingly, Libanius chose a shared *paideia* as common ground between himself and Gamaliel, a distant and formidable Palestinian potentate, a man endowed with an enviable ability to make and break governors. Libanius was concerned, as always, with the smooth working of his own patronage networks. Thus, he urged the patriarch to admit his friend, Philippianus, to the charmed circle of his acquaintances: Philippianus should be 'inscribed on the list of your friends'.[37] A penniless lawyer should have something to put in his purse: 'This, after Tyche, both you and the governor can bring to pass, and you more than the governor.'[38] Libanius' protégé, Theophilus, 'a very wise and just man whose place is among books both when he is awake and sleeping', was presented to the patriarch as a fellow lover of literature.[39] And the 'literature' to which Libanius referred was not Torah. In the letter, Gamaliel is assumed to understand a reference to the proverbial honesty of Aristides, son of Lysimachus. He is asked to 'become an Achilles to Telephus' by helping to 'heal anger with mildness', by bailing out a disgraced governor.[40] If these two men, both in late middle age at that time, felt in any way that they had to make hay while the sun shone, despite the lowering storm-clouds of a Christian empire, Libanius certainly knew how to do this, and did it, with gusto, in the sun of the 'long summer's afternoon of Hellenism', by means of a literary culture magnificently soundproofed to contemporary religious passions.

To a very large extent, then, the history of tolerance and intolerance in the later Roman empire is not to be sought through the examination of a few proof texts, nor can its quality be assessed through a few well-known incidents, admirable or repugnant though these may be. It belongs to the wider topic of the political and cultural factors that went to make up the basically unheroic, but tenacious, moral fibre of the late Roman local elites.

Nothing illustrates this more clearly than do the wider repercussions of the incidents of spectacular violence against pagan temples and Jewish synagogues that emerge in high profile in all Christian narratives of the reign of Theodosius I, from 379 to 395.[41] In this period, violence against pagan sites was widespread. It was purposive and vindictive. The hands and feet of pagan statues were broken; their faces and genitals were mutilated; sacred precincts were 'purged' by fire.[42]

Yet our repelled fascination with such actions should not lead us to amplify them unduly. Deliberate acts of desecration do not necessarily betray the presence of uncontrollable multitudes. They may have been the work of a determined few, briskly performed, possibly even so as to avoid the mobilisation of a larger crowd.

Above all, it is important to stress that we know of many such acts of iconoclasm and arson because well-placed persons still felt free to present these incidents as flagrant departures from a more orderly norm. Libanius did this, in his famous *Oratio pro Templis*, deploring the destruction of the temples in Syria, in 386. The generals in the entourage of Theodosius I were shocked on receiving the news of the burning of the synagogue in Callinicum, in 388, and attempted to shout down Ambrose, when he confronted the emperor Theodosius beside the altar in the Catholic basilica of Milan. The bishop of Callinicum had been on the verge of making reparations for the burning, as he had been commanded to do by the local governor, and would have done so, tamely enough, had Ambrose not intervened in the case. The town-council of Panopolis protested against the depredations of Shenoute of Atripe in the 420s, and succeeded in bringing him to trial.[43]

The fact that vocal protests failed on these occasions does not mean that others did not keep on trying. Beyond the vivid flashes of pagan indignation and of Christian self-justification that light up for us the incidents of violence which occurred in the late fourth and early fifth centuries, it is possible to detect a solid fog-bank of tacit disapproval. The reason is obvious. Spasmodic, largely unpredictable violence of this kind was inconsistent with the perpetual, controlled violence of a heavily governed society. If violence was to happen, it was essential that the traditional elites should not lose the monopoly of such violence. They did not want it to slip into the hands of erratic outsiders.

It may well be for this reason that so many sources presented the Christian monks in disproportionately high relief. To use the memorable characterisation of Libanius: 'This black-robed tribe who eat more than elephants sweep across the countryside like a river in spate . . . and, by ravaging the temples, they ravage the estates.'[44] Libanius appears to a modern reader to be describing a monk-led *Jacquerie*. In fact, he was constructing with his habitual skill a familiar caricature. He brought to bear upon the monks a well-known strategy of Roman invective. The monks were made to appear guilty of *latrocinium*, of *lésteia, mntléstés* (in the succinct Coptic adaptation used in connection with Shenoute): they had resorted to the unsanctioned use of force.[45] As a result, their rowdy activities were invoked to cast a shadow of illegality on what had been, in reality, a thoroughly cold-blooded and orderly affair – the pointed and 'surgical' desecration of active pagan shrines by a Christian Pretorian Prefect on a tour of duty in the eastern provinces. The grass-roots violence of the monks was probably less important than the controlled violence of Theodosius' determination to be finished with paganism. But it was the violence of which one was still free to talk.

Monks figure so largely in accounts such as those of Libanius because theirs was a form of 'deniable' violence. Monks enjoyed no legal status. They were not members of the clergy. One did not have to treat a monk with respect. He was not a *vir venerabilis*, as was the Christian bishop. Often lower class, and frequently strangers in the area, monks could be given a good flogging and run out of town. And this is what happened to many monks, and not least at the hands of Christian bishops. When the monk Hypatius and his companions arrived at Chalcedon (Kadiköy), a fashionable suburb across the water from Constantinople, to protest against the Olympic Games instituted by the Prefect of the City in 434–5, the bishop of Chalcedon simply told him to mind his own business. 'Are you determined to die, even if no one wishes to make a martyr of you? As you are a monk, go and sit in your cell and keep quiet. This is my affair.'[46]

Though placed in the mouth of a Christian bishop, it is the voice of the governing class of the eastern empire as a whole, a class with which bishops had become identified, by birth, culture and autocratic temperament. Such persons remained quietly determined that, if Christianity were to triumph through their authority, they alone should have the monopoly of the force necessary to bring this about.

The determination of the local elites to conduct the Christianisation of the empire on their own terms is shown by the fate of the statues of the gods in this time. So many were preserved.

Indeed, the dramatic narratives that we described in our previous lecture may have made it, if anything, easier to effect a 'laicisation' of the urban landscape in many cities. After the violent public humiliation of the gods who had dwelt in them, temples and statues could be allowed to survive intact as 'ornaments' of their city. No longer associated with the 'contagion' of sacrifice, the shining marble of classical statues was held to have regained a pristine innocence. The idols became what they have remained for us – works of art. It was a situation whose humour was not lost on that wry pagan, Palladas of Alexandria, as he viewed the splendid art gallery set up in the palace of a Christian lady, Marina: 'The inhabitants of Olympus, having become Christians, live here undisturbed: for here, at least, they will escape the cauldron that melts them down for petty change.'[47]

It is typical of the resilience and the all-intrusive presence of such elites that we should know of one of the most bloody clashes between pagans and Christians in North Africa – a riot in which no less than sixty Christians were killed at Sufes, when a statue of Hercules had been overturned – only from a letter written by Augustine. Augustine had been provoked to write a rebuke to the city, because its council, with a stolid sense of its own rights, had insisted that Christians should bear the cost of re-gilding the beard of the overturned statue. It was, after all, so they claimed, still the city's proudest monument![48]

Altogether, these detailed observations, drawn from many areas of the empire, prompt a more general conclusion. The process of Christianisation in the later empire – as, indeed, in later centuries – can never be treated in isolation. Even the most notorious features of this process, on which we have concentrated in this chapter – the religious intolerance that was embraced with such evident gusto by vocal Christian authors, that played so large a part in Christian narratives of the triumph of the Church, and that has tended, as a consequence, to rivet the shocked attention of modern historians of liberal temper, such as ourselves – must be set against as wide a background as possible. Not only in its most flagrant manifestations, but, quite as much, in its innumerable, barely documented, mute restraints, the expression of religious intolerance was part and parcel of the peculiar nature of the exercise of power in late antiquity. Its rhythms were not determined only by what is abundantly documented – by imperial laws, by the utterances of imperious bishops, by the violent actions of monks – but also by the more faceless but, ultimately, decisive determination of the average bearers of authority in late Roman society to remain in control of their own world. The relatively humble details which have claimed our attention in this chapter hint at a wider phenomenon. All over the Mediterranean world, profound religious changes, heavy with potential for violence, were channelled into the more predictable, but no less overbearing 'gentle violence' of a stable social order.

This, in turn, may bring us a little way to explaining a millennium-long change. In the first century AD, a Phrygian gentleman declared, in his last will and testament, that his bequests should stand 'for as long as the eternal dominion of the Romans should last'. At the end of the ninth century AD, an Anglo-Saxon landowner in Kent declared that his will should stand, 'as long as baptism lasts, and money can be raised from the land'.[49] Vastly different from each other as those two gentlemen must have been, they are part of the same continuum. What we call the 'process of Christianisation' can never be divorced from the wider debate on the nature and modes of authority, by which a universal Christian Church insensibly came to replace a universal empire. First the Roman empire, then the Christian Church came to stand for a reassuringly immovable horizon beyond which privileged and settled persons (persons such as those who have figured in this chapter, at the expense of other, better-known because more vocal, participants in the late Roman scene) were frankly disinclined to look. But it is time to leave the well-to-do. In the course of the fifth and sixth centuries, whole populations found their horizon increasingly bounded by the Christian Church. How they were helped, by the vivid figure of the Christian holy man, to bring some form of Christian order to what had remained, for them, a profoundly ambiguous super-natural world, will be the subject of our last chapter.

Chapter 3

ARBITERS OF THE HOLY
the Christian holy man in late antiquity

✠

Some time in the 520s, the great old man Barsanuphius, an Egyptian recluse, wrote from his cell in the vicinity of Gaza, in order to comfort a sick and dispirited monk:

> I speak in the presence of Christ, and I do not lie, that I know a servant of God, in our generation, in the present time and in this blessed place, who can also raise the dead in the name of Jesus our Lord, who can drive out demons, cure the incurable sick, and perform other miracles no less than did the Apostles . . . for the Lord has in all places His true servants, whom He calls no more *slaves* but *sons* [*Galatians* 4:7] . . . If someone wishes to say that I am talking nonsense, as I said, let him say so. But if someone should wish to strive to arrive at that high state, let him not hesitate.[1]

Throughout the Christian world of the fifth and sixth centuries, average Christian believers (like the sick monk, Andrew) were encouraged to draw comfort from the expectation that, somewhere, in their own times, even maybe in their own region, and so directly accessible to their own distress, a chosen few of their fellows (who might be women quite as much as men) had

achieved, usually through prolonged ascetic labour, an exceptional degree of closeness to God. God loved them as His favoured
children. He would answer their prayers on behalf of the majority
of believers, whose own sins kept them at a distance from Him.
Thus, when the bubonic plague struck the eastern Mediterranean
in 542/3, the Great Old Man wrote at once to reassure his monks
on the state of the world:

> There are many who are imploring the mercy of God, and
> certainly no one is more a lover of mankind than He, but He does
> not wish to show mercy, for the mass of sins committed in the
> world stands in His way. There are, however, three men who are
> perfect before God, who have transcended the measure of human
> beings and who have received the power to bind and to loose, to
> remit our faults or to retain them. They *stand upright in the breach*
> [*Psalms* 105:23] to ensure that the world is not wiped out at one
> blow, and, thanks to their prayers, God will chastise with mercy
> . . . They are John, at Rome, Elias, at Corinth, and another in the
> province of Jerusalem. And I am confident that they shall obtain
> that mercy.[2]

Holy persons of this kind came to play a crucial role in the
imagination of many late antique Christians. They made
the Christian God present in their own age and locality; and they
did so to such an extent that disbelief came to focus less on the
existence of the Christian God so much as on His willingness to
lavish on a distant human race – and especially on the unkempt
inhabitants of one's own region – the crowning mercy of palpable
human agents of His will. At the same time as Barsanuphius wrote
his letters, near Gaza, a farmer in the high plateau behind the
coastline of Lycia was unimpressed when told by his neighbour of
visits to the holy man, Nicholas of Sion: 'What is this "servant
of God"? As the Lord God lives, I would not put my trust in any
man on earth.'[3]

Lapidary though such statements of belief and disbelief might be, their very trenchancy served to veil – from contemporaries quite as much as from modern historians – a whole range of less clearly focussed expectations, that surrounded the figure of the holy man in late antiquity. It is to this wider background that I wish to turn in this chapter. I shall attempt to use the vivid material associated with the lives of the major holy men of late antiquity to seize the characteristics of the period as a whole, as one stage among many in the long process of Christianisation.

Before I do this, however, it is as well to begin with a frank admission. I am far less certain than I once was – now over twenty years ago – when I first wrote on 'The Rise and Function of the Holy Man', as to how exactly to fit the holy man into the wider picture of the religious world of late antiquity.

On looking back, I think that, in 1971, I had been content to see him in close up, as it were. In so doing, I was following almost too closely the grain of our principal sources (on which I worked most intensely at that time) – the vivid *Lives* of individual holy men, usually written, by their disciples, after their death. These accounts presented the holy man interacting with all manner of persons. They emphasised specific incidents of healing, good advice, cursing and successful intercession, both with God in heaven and with the powerful on earth. Seen in terms of these sharply delineated actions, the holy man himself is placed, like a figure in a Chinese landscape, against a mist-laden and seemingly measureless background. How to relate foreground and background, the known activities of the holy man with their wider social and religious implications – and hence how to explain their overall significance for contemporaries and their relative importance in relation to other forms of religious activity – is a problem that I did not address as extensively as, perhaps, I should have done in 1971.[4]

Let me try to make good my omissions at that time, by placing the holy man against a wider background. I will deal, first, with the role of the holy man at his least exceptional, as a validator of practices that were widespread within the Christian communities of the time. Then I will suggest some of the ways in which the holy man served a far from Christian world, less, in this chapter, as an arbiter and a patron (as I had done in 1971), than as a rallying-point – a facilitator for the creation of new religious allegiances and of new religious patterns of observance. In so doing, the holy man played an important role as what I would call an 'arbiter of the holy'. In his day-to-day activities, as these were later recorded in his *Life*, he embraced and, eventually, reduced to order the many conflicting systems of explanation that characterised the religious world of late antiquity. Placed between Christian and pagan clients, the holy man aided the emergence of the new, distinctive 'religious commonsense', associated with a more all-embracing and exclusive monotheism, which, as I pointed out in my first chapter, was to prove the most decisive – but, at the time, the most hesitantly arrived at – cognitive change in the late antique and early medieval period.

But let us turn, first, to the foreground – to the holy man in his dealings with other, self-professed Christians. The holy man's activities, though usually presented, in retrospect, in our sources as dramatic and utterly exceptional, were, in reality, no more than a highly visible peak in a spiritual landscape that rose gently upwards from the expectations and activities of ordinary Christians in towns and villages. A community of believers, endowed by baptism with the gift of the Holy Spirit, all Christians were potentially 'holy'. In late antique conditions, this fact was expected to be shown by the possession of spiritual powers. To take one well-known example: Augustine's mother, Monica, took for granted that she would receive God-given, premonitory dreams; and Augustine himself believed that he had been cured of toothache by the prayers of his friends at Cassiciacum, not all of whom had been baptised.[5]

Unassuming and intermittent expectations of help and comfort from religious persons (from women quite as much as from men, and from pious lay persons as much as from the clergy) remained usual in any Christian community. The 'religious person', the *vir religiosus*, the *femina religiosa*, was watched carefully by his or her neighbours, for evidence of virtue and, hence, of spiritual powers that might prove useful to others. A layman complained to Barsanuphius that his retiring disposition, his unwillingness to get involved in local politics and his unusual sexual modesty when visiting the public baths had already given him an embarrassing reputation for being a holy person.[6] The further step, to a demand for a show of spiritual power, was a short one. Faced by a nest of angry wasps, the harvesters of Besne, near Nantes, turned to Friardus, a devout peasant, half in jest and half in earnest: 'Let the religious fellow come, the one who is always praying, who makes the sign of the Cross on his eyes and ears, who crosses himself whenever he goes out of the house.'[7] Only the pious Friardus had the power to halt wasps.

Healing substances also circulated freely. 'Oil of prayer' could be obtained from the lamps around the altar of any number of churches, and might be applied with the prayers of any person with even a moderate reputation for holiness.[8] In his exile in Amaseia (Amasya, Turkey) the patriarch Eutychius of Constantinople settled down, in his monastery, to function in a small way as a wonderworker. A man blinded for perjury was healed by the prayers of Eutychius after three days of anointing with oil. A woman who had difficulties with giving her milk ended up with such an abundant supply that she was able to act as wetnurse to all the children of her neighbourhood.[9]

Believers who went out to a major holy man, such as Symeon Stylites or his sixth-century imitator, Symeon the Younger, opted for a more dramatic solution for their ills. They were prepared to travel considerable distances. They arrived at a site associated, whenever possible, with the wild antithesis to the settled land. They came as pilgrims, to find (in the words of Victor Turner), 'in a "far" milieu, the basic elements and structures of [their] faith in their unshielded, virgin radiance'.[10] But what they usually got, in fact, was 'home cooking'. The supplicants of the great holy men received exactly the same, banal remedies for their ills as circulated at home. But these were now applied by hands known without doubt to be holy, at a place shorn of the disillusionments of everyday life.

The holy man was valued as a more reliable healer and source of comfort than was the average Christian. But a successful holy man was a costly amenity. Holy men and their followers were often settled on marginal lands. In the hey-day of his reputation, each one attracted large bands of disciples and crowds of pilgrims, many of whom stayed for long periods in his presence. If successful, they required permanent facilities – buildings, a water-supply, large surpluses of food and money to give to the poor.

Holy men weighed on the delicate economy of their region. From the autobiography of Valerius of Bierzo, in seventh-century Galicia,[11] through Saint Benedict and his enemy, the priest Florentius, at Subiaco,[12] to the three thousand monks settled in the Judaean desert,[13] the huge convents outside Amida (which were all too easily devastated once the Chalcedonian authorities cut off the surplus of food usually offered to them by a devout laity, by the brutally simple expedient of billeting troops on the region),[14] to Nestorian convents in northern Iraq, regularly pillaged by their Kurdish neighbours,[15] there is hardly an account of the successful establishment of a holy man, and of the monastic complex associated with his person, that is not marked by savage competition for scarce resources, waged between the newcomers and local leaders, clergy and villagers.

In order to survive, holy men were dependent on patronage, and frequently on the crushing patronage of emperors, kings and great landowners. In return, they justified their position by standing, in the eyes of the world, as the quintessence of good patronage. Hence the vividness and the circumstantiality of the accounts which show the holy man rebuking the rich, protecting peasants from extortion, arbitrating in local disputes and facing down high-ranking officials, even the emperor himself, on behalf of the poor, the oppressed and the condemned. It has proved tempting to explain the rise and function of the holy man in terms of the manner in which holy men were believed, by their admirers, to have played the role of 'the "good patron" writ large'. It is a temptation to which I succumbed with gusto in 1971.[16]

In so doing, I now realise that I fell into the trap prepared for their readers by the disciples of the holy man. The posthumous *Lives* of so many holy men were written in large part so as to explain, and to maintain, the wealth of the holy man's establishment. This was no easy task, once the glory of his living presence had departed. The *Lives* achieved their effect through censoring one side of the gift exchange that had taken place around the figure of the holy man – the steady, often disquieting flow of gifts and favours from the outside world that gave the holy man's activities an appropriate degree of splendour and public recognition. At the same time, they consistently presented the holy man's activities in terms of the other side of that gift exchange – the seemingly effortless, 'gravity-free' flow of divine favours that stemmed from his person, in the form of acts of successful arbitration, plainspeaking, cursing and intercession, on behalf of individuals or whole communities.

To take one small, but revealing example: by the 580s, visitors to Symeon the Younger on the *Mons Admirabilis*, the Wonder-Filled Mountain, outside Antioch (the present-day Samandağı, Symeon's Mountain) would have been impressed by a complex of buildings at the foot of the column of the saint, the splendour of whose surviving capitals alone reflected a *koiné* of princely art, that stretched from Constantinople to Kermanshah. Such buildings were notoriously expensive. Yet the biographer of Symeon insisted that they had cost nothing: they were the product of Isaurian stone-masons who had worked solely out of gratitude to the saint, in return for the healings that he had bestowed on them.[17]

In the same way, the wealth associated with the growing establishment of a holy man was usually explained by reference to a series of specific incidents, in which important persons, who stood for the wealth and power of the 'world' in its most obtrusive and darkened form, had been miraculously humbled by the holy man. Wealth that came to the holy man's establishment was rendered clean, in this manner, by a dramatic story in which the original giver of the wealth had first been 'taught a lesson' by the saint.[18]

Altogether, the presentation of the holy man's success in terms of a carefully censored language of 'clean' patronage does not mean that patronage, in itself, explains the prominence of the holy man. I would, rather, spend the remainder of the chapter looking at him less in terms of the clear, beneficial role allotted to him by his late antique biographers, but, rather, from a greater distance, as a figure who, in many regions, acted as a facilitator in the transition from paganism to Christianity. The Christian holy man emerged at a crucial moment in the overall religious history of post-imperial Western Europe and the Byzantine Middle East. He was a figure of genuine spiritual power at a time when the holy still stretched far beyond the somewhat narrow confines of the triumphant Christian church.

The chronology of the emergence of major holy figures seems to indicate that this was so. Christian narratives of triumph, as we have seen in the first chapter, tended to suspend the sense of time. They emphasised the instantaneous nature of victory over the gods, associated with the destruction of a shrine, the arrival of a preacher, the establishment of a church or monastery. They deliberately looked through the long periods of waiting – the spiritual convalescence of whole regions, the adjustment of villagers to a world without public gods, the barely documented contacts between non-Christians and Christians through marriage, through trade and immigration, even through the unspectacular, or downright suspect, ministrations of occasional itinerant preachers. What we often call the 'Christianisation' of an area, in late antiquity and in the early middle ages, is often no more than a final painting up, in the vivid colours of an acceptable ecclesiastical narrative, of a situation that had already been sketched out, in full, in shades of grey. The lives of Christian holy men are so precious to us, in late antiquity, because they are one of the few sources that take us a little closer to that grey time.

It is no coincidence, for instance, that a figure of the stature of Symeon Stylites should have appeared when he did in northern Syria. The ecclesiastical structures of the region had been in place for some generations. The pagan temples had been officially closed for a quarter of a century. But a strong form of local religious leadership had not yet arisen to negotiate an honourable surrender for the gods. This was what Symeon did. Firmly placed on a column, which, in itself, may have linked his person to ancient memories of holy stones,[19] administering banal and widely recognised forms of blessing (the *hnana* of the dust from the sacred enclosure beneath his column), summoning local church congregations, through their priests, to what amounted to gigantic 'revivalist' meetings associated with Christian penitential supplication, Symeon stood on the low slopes of the limestone ridge, as a highly personalised challenge to the ancient pilgrimage site on top of Sheikh Barakat. Despite the splendid buildings that were lavished on it after his death, it is not the relatively low-lying area of Telnesin, but the conical shape of Sheikh Barakat that still catches the eye of the traveller in the Jebel Sem'an, as it towers with an immemorial sacrality above the plain of Dana. Placed, in this manner, in the shadow of an ancient sacred place, Symeon negotiated many surrenders of the gods. Beduin tribesmen burned their idols in his presence.[20] Whole villages entered into a 'covenant' with him. A polytheist village in the mountains of Lebanon was told that if they followed his commands, by placing stones carved with the sign of the cross, or blessed by portions of his holy dust, on the four corners of their fields, and if they destroyed their shrines and household idols, they would enjoy protection from creatures of the wild – from werewolves and from ravenous field mice.[21]

It was possible to give way with good grace to such persons. Their presence in the neighbourhood introduced an element of consent into an otherwise abrasive process, habitually marked by desecrated shrines and by the forced abandonment of ancient public rites. When the formidable Shenoute of Atripe prophesied to the villagers of Sment, in Upper Egypt, that they would lose their gods, they knew enough about the 'process of Christian-isation' to assume the worst: 'A governor will surely come and will oppress us.'[22] Instead they got Apa Moyses, whose violence, though spectacular and disastrous for their temples, partook in an ancient language of the sacred, which rendered defeat, if not palatable, at least meaningful. For, unlike a governor, Moyses knew something about the supernatural. He could be accepted as an expert in the ways of a new god, before whose presence the ancient powers of the region had, apparently, withdrawn, if only for a time.

Unlike the European missionaries of a later age, the Christian holy men and women of late antiquity and the early middle ages, to use the words of Kaplan's study of the holy men of medieval Ethiopia, 'appeared as representatives of a power superior to that of traditional faiths, but not as purveyors of a dramatically different world view or type of religion'.[23] Filled with the Holy Spirit and more certain than were most other Christians of enjoying the support of a whole hierarchy of heavenly powers, in alliance with whom they upheld the claims of Christ, their God, holy men (unlike most of us who study them) knew spiritual power when they saw it. They frequently engaged it at dangerously close quarters. Long and intimate duels with the local sorcerer were almost *de rigueur* in the life of a successful saint.[24] Sometimes one even senses that the one is a doublet, rather than an enemy, of the other. For what historians of religion have often described as 'syncretism', and what historians of the Church tend to dismiss as forms of 'semi-paganism', were never the mindless process that such descriptions imply. Far from being locked into an inert system of traditional beliefs, that continued largely unchanged in thinly disguised Christian form, late antique pagans were active persons. They lived with alert confidence in the rustling world of invisible powers, the *mundus*, whose powerful, diffuse sacrality we have encountered in the first chapter. They were impenitent *bricoleurs*. Hackers of the supernatural, they were quite prepared to 'cannibalise' Christian belief and practice, in order to find spare parts with which to enrich their own religious systems. When we get close to a holy man, it is often possible to glimpse, in the penumbra of his reputation, a busy world of cultic experimentation which, though disapproved of in our sources as the work of rivals, had, in fact, incorporated crucial elements of the Christian saint's own thought world. To take one example, at Néris, in Berry, Patroclus found himself faced, at the time of the bubonic plague of 571, by a woman, Leubella, who had received healing tokens from the devil, 'falsely appearing [to her] as saint Martin . . . [bearing] offerings [of objects] which would, he said, save the people'. But Patroclus himself was also acutely aware of the need for supernatural measures in a time of crisis. He had almost succumbed to the temptation to come down from the hills to save the people as a wonderworker. Only after he had received a vision of the 'abominations' of the world to which he had been tempted to return, did he go back to his cell, to find a mysterious object – 'a tile on which was the sign of the Lord's cross': that is, an object offered by the true God, that mirrored exactly the occult tokens paraded by a local religious figure.[25]

Not surprisingly in such a situation, no small part of the work of late antique hagiography was the attempt to bring order to a supernatural world shot through with acute ambiguity, characterised by uncertainty as to the meaning of so many manifestations of the holy, and, as a result, inhabited by religious entrepreneurs of all faiths. For this reason, we should not underestimate the importance of the stereotyped and repetitive quality of so many of the incidents that were narrated in the lives of Christian holy men. As a recent study of the working of social memory has made plain, such frequently repeated stories 'provide us with a set of stock explanations which underly our predisposition to interpret reality in the ways that we do'.[26] In a world where reality was constantly being interpreted in very different ways, by differing groups, the central narratives that constantly recur in Christian hagiography played a major role in the creation of a specifically Christian form of religious 'common sense'. They caught the holy in a fine web of Christian words.

Late antique persons, of every class and level of culture, lived in many conflicting 'thought-worlds'.[27] Potentially exclusive explanatory systems coexisted in their minds. The host of the monk, Peter the Iberian, an eminent Egyptian, was a good Christian; but he was also 'caught in the error of pagan philosophers, whose ideas he loved greatly'.[28] He employed a magician to cure his daughter. Nor did these systems only run parallel to each other. They frequently interlocked as separate parts within a single process of cure. A notable of Alexandria went to the healing shrine of Saints Cyrus and John, to receive a cure from their hands. But he claimed to have done so 'in order that his horoscope should be fulfilled'.[29]

Holy men themselves were frequently less tidy, in practice, in their choice of explanatory systems than were their biographers, in retrospect. Indeed, a very large part of their appeal, as facilitators of religious change, lay in the fact that they were thought to be able to embrace and validate a wide range of potentially exclusive explanatory systems. They belonged to a category of persons who were assumed, by their supplicants, to have access to knowledge of the holy in all its manifestations. Such expectations committed them to activities that ranged far beyond an exclusively Christian art of prayer. A respected Christian saint was a person who had been allowed to have the last word in what had been a long and well-informed discussion of supernatural causality, in which many other experts had participated. When Theodore of Symeon was conceived, his mother, Maria, dreamed that a brilliant star had descended into her womb. Her lover (an acrobatic camel-rider on an imperial mission) was delighted. She would have a baby boy, he said, who would become a bishop. Next, Maria went to a holy man with second sight in a neighbouring village. He concurred. 'A star', he told her, 'is held to signify the glory of an emperor by those who are expert in interpreting visions; but with you it must not mean this.' Also consulted by Maria, the bishop of Anastasioupolis, 'by God's inspiration, gave her the same interpretation'.[30] When Theodore, sure enough, grew up to be both a bishop and a holy man, he functioned in a similar manner. As a representative of the loving-kindness of God, he embraced and validated all forms of useful knowledge: 'if any required medical treatment for certain illnesses or surgery or a purging draught or hot springs, this God-inspired man would prescribe the best thing for each, for even in technical matters he had become an experienced doctor . . . and he would always state clearly which doctor they should employ'.[31]

Nor did the information flow only in one direction, from a holy man to his clients. Viewing the crowds of sufferers around the shrine of Saint Epiphanius at Salamis, in the early seventh century, a 'philosopher' informed the bishop that the majority of those present would be cured by a simple change in diet. Responsible for the success of a crowded healing establishment, the bishop agreed. The philosopher's remedy worked wonders.[32]

We should never forget the freedom of manœuvre that late Roman persons continued to enjoy, within the interstices of the many explanatory systems that jostled each other in the back of their minds. Occasionally we come upon a precious moment when a community, as a whole, was forced to decide on the meaning of an apparently supernatural event. When, in 420, the monk Fronto challenged local noble families and clergy, at Tarragona, on an inconclusive charge of sorcery, a servant of Count Asterius burst into the crowded basilica with an armed retinue. Pointing at Fronto, he roared: 'Give me that dog. I will stop his barking . . . ' That evening, the servant died of a stroke.

When this happened, all the faithful, frightened by the obvious power of this sign, ceased to attack me for a little while. But my enemies and the Count's whole household . . . demanded that I be punished as a murderer, since I had killed a man with death-dealing spells. There were even a few of those, totally lacking in faith, who said that it had all happened by coincidence.[33]

Such uncertainty was not surprising. For many late antique Christians, the sacred had remained profoundly faceless and ill defined. Illusion was always possible. The Great Old Men of the desert had fostered a view of the untransformed human consciousness as a fragile thing, perpetually ringed by demonic mirages. The demons were the lords of illusion. In dreams the demons might even take the form of holy figures, Barsanuphius told a worried layman: only the sign of the cross was reliable; for the demons could not bring themselves to imitate it.[34]

The power of the demons, and the lengthening shadow cast across the world by the approach of Antichrist, had led mankind into a perpetual twilight. It was barely possible to discriminate between holiness and illusion. In the 430s, a monk appeared in Carthage. He applied to the sick, oil poured over the bone of a martyr. 'He brought hallucinations to play on the blind and the sick . . . so that they thought that they had recovered their sight and ability to walk. But in departing from him, the illnesses in whose grip they were held remained.'[35] He left the city in a hurry. Yet just such cures, also performed with the 'oil of saints', only a generation later, made the reputation of Daniel, a Syrian recluse, and later a famous stylite, established beside the busy ferry across the Bosphorus (near Arnavutköy and Rumeli Hıssar) a little to the north of Constantinople.[36]

Perpetually haunted in this way by ambiguity, belief was never an easy matter, even at the best of times. In times of acute crisis, Christian explanatory systems collapsed like a house of cards. A massive public catastrophe, such as the onslaught of the plague, swamped the ministrations of the holy man. It was reassuring to believe that the cloth from the tomb of Saint Remigius, carried in a litter around Rheims, had created a sacred circuit that kept the bubonic plague away from the city.[37] But Rheims was fortunate. Far from the Mediterranean, the more erratic movements of the disease could be held within a conventional Christian narrative. When the plague first struck the eastern Mediterranean, with devastating effect, in 542, resort to the prayers of the saints was not the only, indeed, nor the first reflex of the afflicted populations. Demons in the form of angels appeared in Palestine, urging the inhabitants of one city to resume the worship they had once paid to a prominent bronze statue. Elsewhere, the word got round that 'If one throws pots out of the house the plague will leave the city.' It became unsafe to walk in the streets by reason of the crockery raining down from every window.[38]

It is in reading such accounts that we realise how little, in fact, of the public space of late Roman society had come to be occupied by Christian holy persons. The solid gold of demonstrative Christian sanctity was spectacular; but it circulated in strictly delimited channels, in what had remained, to an overwhelming extent, a supernatural 'subsistence economy', accustomed to handling life's doubts and cares according to more old-fashioned and low-key methods.

To take one example: in the theological controversies that rocked the eastern empire in the fifth and sixth centuries, Christian holy men played an important role in the mobilisation of local opinion on either side – all the more so as many influential lay persons made a habit of taking the Eucharist only from the 'blessed' hands of known holy men.[39] But their opinions on theology carried little weight with the experts. Considering a theological dictum ascribed to Saint Spyridion of Cyprus, the great Monophysite theologian, Severus of Antioch, observed drily that, while Spyridion may have received the 'gift of healing', the holy old man had evidently not received the 'gift of wisdom'.[40]

Deeply conscious of the ambiguity of the sacred and fully aware of the limits of its field of action in a complex world, the society that turned to Christian holy persons was more niggardly than our hagiographic sources might lead us, at first sight, to suppose, in lavishing credulity upon them. But when they did, they were encouraged to 'stylise' their imagination of the workings of the supernatural in a highly specific way. The holy man was a 'servant' of his God. He was also a 'patron' in that he offered petitions to God on behalf of others. His actions assumed, at a profound level, that the events of this world were the product of conflicting wills (in which conflict, the supremely wilful envy of the demons played a crucial role), and that true order meant the ultimate submission of all wills to God, the supreme ruler of the universe.

The intimacy of holy persons with their Lord could be as tender as that of a son, of a familiar friend, even of a lover. But the overwhelming weight of language, in our texts, presented the holy man in his public *persona* as a courtier and a patron. For many regions, this attitude involved far more than an unthinking projection on to the invisible world of the observed working of patronage in the highly centralised court-society of the later Roman empire. To see the invisible world in such clear-cut terms involved making a conscious choice between available religious traditions. The supernatural world did not always work in an up-to-date, late Roman manner. In 370, Athanasius wrote that, of course, dreams of the future were vouchsafed to Christian devotees at the shrines of the martyrs. What mattered was how this happened. Many Egyptian Christians seem to have assumed that the martyrs, as 'unconquered' heroes who had overcome the demons of the lower air by their heroic deaths, could now be prevailed upon, by the prayers of believers, to torture the demons yet further (in a long Egyptian tradition, by which higher gods bullied and threatened their subordinates) to reveal their own, unearthly knowledge of the future. In was not like that, Athanasius insisted. God sent the dreams because the martyrs had acted as ambassadors – *etreupresbeue*: they had presented the prayers of the faithful to His court.[41]

The language of patronage at a distant court, though it became predominant in this period, needed constant fine-tuning. Replication of existing social structures had its limits when describing the invisible world. An Egyptian bishop condemned the 'simple folk' who believed, on the strength of an 'imperial' model of the supernatural world, that the Archangel Michael, rather than having been forever present in his mighty role from the first dawn of Creation, had, so they believed, ousted Satan in a *coup d'état* in the Palace of Heaven; and consequently that, like any other Roman consul, Michael was obliged to scatter the benefits of healing upon his people on the day of his festival. For this was the day when he had received, from God, the formal scroll of his appointment![42]

The emphasis on the interaction of free wills implied in the model of intercession in the court of heaven brought a quality of mercy into an otherwise inflexible and potentially profoundly impersonal *cosmos*. And with the notion of freedom came also the notion of sin. The holy man was not only a favoured courtier of his God; he was a preacher of repentance. Dramatic changes in health; dramatic changes in the weather; dramatic shifts in the locus of wealth – as gold, precious objects, robes, land, even small children passed from the 'world' to the monastic establishments associated with holy persons: all these highly visible changes were held to have registered the most amazing of all discontinuities – the stirring to contrition of the sinful human heart.

The great *Lives* of the holy men leave us in no doubt as to that basic Christian narrative. It did not coincide with other notions of the sacred that were widespread at the time. Some time after the middle of the fifth century, Athens was afflicted by a drought. Rising to the occasion, the great non-Christian philosopher, Proclus, brought down the rain. The mysterious drone of the sacred bull-roarer, swung above the city by the wise man, restored the burning elements to their harmonious pitch. Himself already something of a lesser god, Proclus' soul was coopted, through these rites, into the quiet and immemorial routine of government, by which the presiding spirits of a small part of the *cosmos* nurtured the sweet air of his beloved Attica.[43] For a moment, Proclus had joined himself to the loving care of the gods; he did not bow, as a courtier and a sinner, before the sole emperor of heaven.

A few decades earlier, drought had fallen, also, on the region of Jerusalem. The processions of Christian villagers, bearing crosses and chanting *Kyrie eleison*, that converged on the monastery of the great Euthymius were treated to a very different view of the universe.

'God, Who fashioned us, is good and benevolent, and *his pity extends over all his works.* But [Euthymius added] *our sins stand between us and Him* . . . This is why in His anger He has brought this correction upon us, so that, disciplined by it, and bettered by repentance, we may approach Him in fear and He accordingly may hear us.' On hearing this, they all cried out in unison. 'You yourself, venerable father, must entreat God for us.' [Euthymius then] went into his oratory without making any promises. Casting himself on his face, he begged God with tears to have mercy on

His creation . . . As he was praying, there suddenly blew up a south wind, the sky was filled with clouds, heavy rain descended and there was a great storm.[44]

Dramatic though such scenes of intercession might be, they did not exhaust expectations of the Christian holy man. Behind the standard, workaday Christian version of a universe made intelligible in terms of sin, affliction and repentance, there always shimmered the majesty of Paradise regained – that is, an image not only of a God placated by bursts of human prayer and contrition, offered to Him on behalf of others by His favoured servants, but of an entire world rejoicing in the recovery of its lost order. In large areas of eastern Christianity (and, if in a more diffident and spasmodic manner, also in the West) the holy man was thought to have brought back to the settled world, from his long sojourn in the wilderness, a touch of the haunting completeness of Adam.[45] Nature, characterised by great, antithetical categories, fell into place around him. On his pillar at Telnesin, Symeon radiated an order that seeped from his person, standing in prayer before the court of God, into the column itself and the sacred space around it. Symeon maintained, as if in microcosm, the fundamental boundaries on which all civilised life was held to depend throughout the Near East.[46] The clutter of stuffed deer, lions and snakes, that lay as ex-votos at the foot of Symeon's column, spoke of notable breaches in the boundary between the animal and the human world healed in the name of the saint.[47] Further from Telnesin, the blessing of Symeon on the crosses set up in his name around villages in the mountains of Lebanon maintained the boundaries of the settled land against the encroaching disorder of the wild woods. The sexes, also, were held apart. In the women's enclosure at the foot of the terrain that rose towards the column, a large female snake was believed to have taken her place, along with the five wives of a visiting Yemeni sheikh, demurely receiving her *hnana*, not from the hands of Symeon, but from the mouth of her male companion.[48]

Symeon was very much a 'revivalist' in a Syrian tradition of Christianity, that had always been marked by a strong sense of cosmic order and with a consequent concern for the proper separation of the sexes. But an Adam might also pass beyond, as well as reinforce, boundaries that bulked so large in the minds of contemporaries. Even the charged barriers between the sexes might open at his touch. When Sabas passed through Scythopolis, in 531–2, his attention was drawn to a woman who lay in the colonnade of the main street, isolated even from her fellow-beggars by the stench of an uncontrolled menstrual haemorrhage. 'He came over to her in the colonnade and said , , , "This my hand I lend to you, and I trust in the God that I worship that you will be cured." Taking the saint's hand, she applied it to the hidden part, and immediately the flux of blood ceased.'[49] By such persons, the 'world' itself – that dark place of 'abominations' so often decried in the monastic literature of the time – was healed. In this sense, the holy man came to be seen as a truly 'angelic' figure. Like the towering angels, he raised his eyes from his clamorous supplicants to contemplate the rich earth, teeming with the possibilities of life. He was not merely a patron surrounded by his human clients. He was responsible to God for all created things. Shenoute was able to stir the tardy Nile to give life, once again, to the land of Egypt; and he did so, not simply as a favoured courtier of God, but, with an ancient congruence, by first making the life-giving liquid of his tears fall on the dead sand of his desert retreat beyond the White Monastery.[50]

Christian holy persons had been shot into prominence, at this time, by an exceptionally stern and world-denying streak in late antique Christianity. Those who approached them, and those who remembered their activities, habitually assumed that they would act upon the spiritual world largely in terms of expectations that echoed all that was most abrasively up-to-date in the hierarchical and patronage-ridden social structure of the later Roman empire. Yet, by sharing, through their prayers, in the concerns of the mighty angels, Christian holy persons had come to embrace the *mundus*, the material world itself. They cradled it, in the Christian imagination, in terms that did better justice, than did an image of their efficacy modelled on human social relations alone, to the notion of a God who loved His own Creation, and so to the tenacious hopes of an overwhelmingly agrarian society locked in the tyrannical, warm embrace of the earth. By their intercessions, the Christian holy men joined with Saint Michael the Archangel, to look with mercy on humanity in all its joys and cares:

> [on] the strenuous work of our hands . . . the quietness of the oxen and the growth of the lambs . . . the wool of the sheep and the milk of the goats . . . the growth of all the fruits of the field . . . the body of the vine and the fullness [which is] in the vine . . . the fatness and the savour of the olives . . . the union of holy matrimony, wherein men beget their children for a blessing . . . in war that destroyeth the ungodly, and establisheth peace, and delivereth the righteous . . . in the midst of the brethren [who live together] . . . and towards those who are weary, and when he giveth them strength.[51]

By playing a role in the slow emergence of an imaginative model of the world that had a place for such wide-arching prayers, the Christian saints of late antiquity helped to make Christianity at last, and for a short moment, before the rise of Islam, the one truly universal religion of much of Europe and the Middle East.

Notes

I CHRISTIANISATION: *narratives and processes*

1 R. S. O. Tomlin, 'The Curse Tablets', in *The Temple of Sulis Minerva at Bath* II, ed. B. Cunliffe (Oxford, 1988), p. 233; see now J. N. Adams, *Britannia* 23 (1992), p. 11.

2 F. Thélamon, *Païens et chrétiens au ive siècle: l'apport de l''Histoire ecclésiastique' de Rufin d'Aquilée* (Paris, 1981) is a model study of one such author.

3 P. Chuvin, *A Chronicle of the Last Pagans* (Cambridge, Mass., 1990): the title of the third chapter.

4 Jacob of Sarug, *On the Fall of the Idols*, 180, transl. S. Landersdorfer, *Ausgewählte Schriften der syrischen Dichter* (Munich, 1913), p. 416.

5 Thélamon, *Païens et chrétiens*, p. 252.

6 Chuvin, *Chronicle of the Last Pagans*, pp. 67–8.

7 J. Geffcken, *The Last Days of Greco-Roman Paganism*, transl. Sabine MacCormack (Amsterdam, 1978) and R. McMullen, *Christianizing the Roman Empire* (New Haven, Conn., 1984) provide fully documented overviews, as do the classic essays in *The Conflict of Paganism and Christianity in the Fourth Century AD*, ed. Arnaldo Momigliano (Oxford, 1963).

8 Thélamon, *Païens et chrétiens*, p. 227; see now E. Wipszycka, 'La Christianisation de l'Egypte au ive–ve siècles', *Aegyptus* 68 (1988), pp. 117–64.

9 Carlo Ginzburg, *Storia notturna: una decifrazione del sabba* (Turin, 1989), pp. 70–88; English transl. *Ecstasies* (New York, 1991), pp. 94–110.

10 R. Macmullen, 'What Difference Did Christianity Make?', *Historia* 35

(1986), pp. 322–43, now in *Changes in the Roman Empire* (Princeton, NJ, 1990), pp. 142–55.

11 R. Lane Fox, *Pagans and Christians* (New York, 1987), p. 21.

12 A. J. Festugière, *La révélation d'Hermès Trismégiste II: le Dieu cosmique* (Paris, 1949), p. 343.

13 *Consultationes Zacchaei Ap;ollonii*, 1.1, ed. G. Morin (Bonn, 1935), p. 8.

14 Augustine, *Sermo*, 18.1.

15 Augustine, *Enarratio I in Ps. 34*, 7.

16 Shenoute, *Contra Origenistas*, 256–7, ed. Tito Orlandi (Rome, 1985), pp. 18–19.

17 Shenoute, *Contra Origenistas*, 821, ed. Orlandi, pp. 62–3.

18 C. Geertz, *Local Knowledge* (New York, 1983), p. 124.

19 L. Schneider, *Die Domäne als Weltbild: Wirkungsstrukturen der spätantiken Bildersprache* (Wiesbaden, 1983).

20 M. Meslin, *La fête des Kalendes de janvier dans l'empire romain* (Brussels, 1970).

21 S. G. MacCormack, *Art and Ceremony in Late Antiquity* (Berkeley, Calif., 1981); Averil Cameron, 'The Construction of Court Ritual: The Byzantine *Book of Ceremonies*', in *Rituals of Royalty, Power, and Ceremonial in Traditional Societies*, ed. David Cannadine and Simon Price (Cambridge, 1987), pp. 106–36.

22 Averil Cameron, *Christianity and the Rhetoric of Empire: The Development of Christian Discourse* (Berkeley, Calif., 1991), pp. 47–88.

23 Alan Cameron, 'Filocalus and Melania', *Classical Philology* 87 (1992), pp. 140–4.

24 M. Salzman, *On Roman Time: The Codex-Calendar of 354* (Berkeley, Calif., 1990).

25 Kathleen Shelton, 'Roman Aristocrats, Christian Commissions: The Carrand Diptych', in *Tradition and Innovation in Late Antiquity*, ed. F. M. Clover and R. S. Humphreys (Madison, Wisc., 1989), pp. 105–27.

26 Schneider, *Domäne als Weltbild*, p. 314; J. G. Deckers, 'Dionysos der Erlöser?', *Römische Quartalschrift* 81 (1986), pp. 145–72.

27 G. W. F. Hegel, *Ästhetik*, 1.1, *Werke*, 10.1 (Berlin, 1835), p. 135.

28 On attitudes to the adoration of imperial images, see *Consultationes Zacchaei et Apollonii*, 1.28, ed. Morin, pp. 34–5, with the commentary of J.-L. Feiertag, *Les Consultationes Zacchaei et Apollonii* (Fribourg-en-Suisse, 1990), pp. 68–97.

29 H. Dessau, *Inscriptiones Latinae Selectae* 8730 (Berlin, 1892), III, p. 983.

30 M. Mundell, 'The Sevso Treasure Hunting Plate', *Apollo*, July 1990, pp. 2–11 and 65–7.

31 Richard Gordon, 'The Veil of Power: Emperors, Sacrificers and Benefactors', in *Pagan Priests*, ed. M. Beard and J. North (Ithaca, NY, 1990), pp. 217–19.

32 *De circensibus*, Codex Salmasianus 197, ed. *Anthologia Latina* I (Leipzig, 1964), p. 161; Ausonius, *Carm.* II.5 – on the Kalends.

33 Y.-M. Duval, 'Des Lupercales de Constantinople aux Lupercales de Rome', *Revue des Etudes Latines* 55 (1977), pp. 222–70, at pp. 236–41.

34 Meslin, *La fête des Kalendes de janvier*, pp. 51–93.

35 Petrus Chrysologus, *Sermo*, 155 bis, I, ed. A. Olivar, *Corpus Christianorum* 24B (Turnhout, 1975), p. 967.

36 Robert Markus, *The End of Ancient Christianity* (Cambridge, 1990), pp. 1–17.

37 Eusebius, *Life of Constantine*, 4.10 – Constantine's letter to Shapur. When serving under Julian the Apostate, the future emperor Valentinian I was believed to have cut off that part of his cloak on which drops of pagan lustral water had been sprinkled: Sozomen, *Historia Ecclesiastica*, VI.6.

38 Augustine, *Enarr. II in Ps. 88*, 14.

39 Augustine, *Epp.*, 46 and 47.

40 *Codex Theodosius*, 9.16.2.

41 Augustine, *De divinatione daemonum*, 2.5; Anastasius Sinaita, *Quaestiones*, 20, *Patrologia Graeca*, 89.524–5.

42 Council of Elvira, canon 41, ed. E. J. Jonkers, *Acta et symbola concilorum quae quarto saeculo habita sunt* (Leiden, 1974), p. 14.

43 Neil McLynn, *Ambrose of Milan: Church and Court in a Christian Capital* (Berkeley, Calif., 1994) now presents a very different Ambrose. The processes to which I refer are best illustrated in the regional treatment of R. Lizzi, 'Ambrose's Contemporaries and the Christianisation of Northern Italy', *Journal of Roman Studies* 80 (1990), pp. 156–73.

44 Markus, *The End of Ancient Christianity*, pp. 107–23; F. Dolbeau, 'Nouveaux sermons de S. Augustin sur la conversion des païens et des donatistes (II)', *Revue des Etudes Augustiniennes* 37 (1991), pp. 37–78 and 'Nouveaux sermons (IV)', *Recherches Augustiniennes* 26 (1992), pp. 69–141.

45 Augustine, *Enarr. I in Ps. 34*, 7.

46 Augustine, *Sermo*, 62.6.10; see F. M. Clover, 'Felix Karthago', in *Tradition and Innovation in Late Antiquity*, pp. 129–62.

47 Augustine, *Sermo*, 198.3.

48 Augustine, *Enarr. II in Ps. 93*, 3.

49 Augustine, *Sermo*, 198.3; see now Dolbeau, 'Nouveaux sermons (IV)', p. 92, for the full context of the passage.

50 John Cassian, *Collationes*, 18.5.23; Sulpicius Severus, *Chronicon*, II:32;

Jerome, *Vita Malchi*, 1; Isidore of Pelusium, *Epp.*, 11.54 and 246, with Markus, *The End of Ancient Christianity*, pp. 166–7.
51 *Consultationes Zacchaei et Apollonii*, 1:28, ed. Morin, p. 35.
52 Augustine, *Ep.*, 29.8–9.
53 *Sermo de saltationibus respuendis. Patrologia Latina: Supplementum* 4.974.
54 E.g. Theodoret, *Curatio affectionum graecarum*, x.80, ed. P. Canivet, *Théodoret de Cyr: thérapeutique des maladies hélléniques*, Sources chrétiennes 57 (Paris, 1958), p. 385; cf. viii.68, p. 335; Christian Gnilka, *Chrêsis: die Methode der Kirchenväter im Umgang mit der antiken Kultur* (Basel and Stuttgart, 1984), pp. 134–40.
55 Øystein Hjort, 'Augustus Christianus – Livia Christiana: *Sphragis* and Roman Portrait Sculpture', in *Aspects of Late Antiquity and Early Byzantium*, ed. L. Ryden and J. O. Rosenqvist (Stockholm, 1993), pp. 99–112.

2 THE LIMITS OF INTOLERANCE

1 G. R. Elton, 'Introduction', *Persecution and Toleration*, Studies in Church History 21, ed. W. J. Shiels (Oxford, 1984), p. xiii.
2 Peter Garnsey, 'Religious Toleration in Classical Antiquity', in *Persecution and Toleration*, pp. 1-27.
3 *Ibid.* p. 1.
4 *Ibid.* p. 6.
5 *Ibid.* p. 12.
6 *Ibid.* p. 16.
7 F. Paschoud, 'L'intolérance chrétienne vue et jugée par les païens', *Cristianesimo nella Storia* 11 (1990), pp. 545–77.
8 Paschoud, 'L'intolérance chrétienne', pp. 549 and 554.
9 Robert L. Wilken, *John Chrysostom and the Jews* (Berkeley, Calif., 1983), pp. 32–3; John Matthews, *The Roman Empire of Ammianus* (London, 1989), pp. 435–51.
10 Rufinus, *Historia Ecclesiastica*, 2.19, *Patrologia Latina* 21.526B.
11 Zosimus, *Historia Nova*, 4.59; see W. Goffart, 'Zosimus, the First Historian of Rome's Fall', *American Historical Review* 76 (1971), pp. 412–41, in *Rome's Fall and After* (London, 1989), pp. 81–110; Kenneth H. Sacks, 'The Meaning of Eunapius' History', *History and Theory* 25 (1986), pp. 52–67; H. Speck, 'Wie dumm darf Zosimos sein? Vorschläge zu seiner Neubewertung', *Byzantinoslavica* 52 (1991), pp. 1–14; G. Fowden, 'The Last Days of Constantine: Oppositional Versions and their Influence', *Journal of Roman Studies* (1994).

12 *Novella Theodosii II*, 3.10. M. Salzman, 'The Evidence for the Conversion of the Roman Empire', *Historia* 42 (1993), pp. 362–78; D. Hunt, 'Christianising the Roman Empire: The Evidence of the Code', in *The Theodosian Code*, ed. J. Harries and I. Wood (London, 1993), pp. 143–58; S. Bradbury, 'Constantine and the Problem of Anti-Pagan Legislation in the Fourth Century', *Classical Philology* 89 (1994), pp. 120–39; M. T. Fögen, *Die Enteignung der Wahrsager* (Frankfurt-on-Main, 1993) – an important study.

13 Peter Brown, *The Body and Society* (New York, 1988), p. 180; Peter Brown, *Power and Persuasion: Towards a Christian Empire* (Madison, Wisc., 1992), pp. 62–3.

14 Porphyry, *De Abstinentia*, 1.1 and 3.

15 Themistius, *Oratio*, 5.67c, ed. G. Downey (Leipzig, 1965), p. 99.

16 C. Andresen, *Nomos und Logos* (Berlin, 1955); Porphyry, apud Eusebius *Praeparatio Evangelica*, 1.2.1–4; K. Strobel, *Das Imperium Romanum im 3. Jahrhundert* (Stuttgart, 1993), pp. 328–40.

1/ Themistius, *Oratio*, 5.69a, ed. Downey, p. 101; Sozomen, *Historia Ecclesiastica*, 6.36.

18 Gregory Nazianzenus, *Oratio*, 28.12 *Patrologia Graeca*, 36.40–1; G. Dagron, 'L'empire romain de l'Orient au ive siècle et les traditions politiques de l'héllénisme', *Travaux et Mémoires* 3 (1968), p. 171, n. 128.

19 Brown, *Power and Persuasion*, pp. 68–70.

20 Themistius, *Oratio*, 8, 113a–115d, ed. Downey, pp. 170–3; Peter Heather, *Goths and Romans, 332–489* (Oxford, 1991), pp. 117–19.

21 Rochelle Snee, 'Valens' Recall of the Nicene Exiles and Anti-Arian Propaganda', *Greek, Roman and Byzantine Studies* 26 (1985), pp. 395–419.

22 Paul Veyne, *Le pain et le cirque* (Paris, 1976), p. 638, transl. as *Bread and Circuses* (London, 1990), p. 361.

23 Brown, *Power and Persuasion*, pp. 20–34; Jean Durliat, *Les finances publiques de Dioclétien aux Carolingiens*, Beihefte der Francia 21 (Sigmaringen, 1990), pp. 13–37.

24 *Vita Porphyrii*, 41, ed. H. Grégoire and M. A. Kugener, *Marc la Diacre: vie de Porphyre* (Paris, 1930), p. 35. Cf. Shenoute, *Ep.* 27, ed. J. Leipoldt and W. Crum, *Corpus Scriptorum Orientalium 43: Scriptores Coptici*, 3 (Leipzig, 1898), p. 88.14.

25 *Collectio Casinensis*, 211, ed. E. Schwartz, *Acta Conciliorum Oecumenicorum*, 1.4 (Berlin, 1932–3), p. 155.

26 Libanius, *Ep.* 1441.

27 A. F. Norman, 'Libanius: The Teacher in an Age of Violence', *Libanios*, ed. G. Fatouros and T. Krischer, Wege der Forschung 621 (Darmstadt, 1983), p. 362.

28 Claude Lepelley, 'Trois documents méconnus sur l'histoire sociale et religieuse de l'Afrique romaine, retrouvés parmi les *Spuria* de Sulpice Sévère', *Antiquités Africaines* 25 (1989), pp. 235–62.

29 *Ibid.*. p. 252.

30 *Codex Theodosianus*, 16.5.52.

31 Augustine, *Ep.* 20*.10, *Bibliothèque augustinienne* 46B (Paris, 1987), p. 308.

32 Brown, *Power and Persuasion*, pp. 59–60.

33 Socrates, *Historia Ecclesiastica*, 7.29.

34 Sebastian Castellio, *Concerning Heretics*, transl. R. H. Bainton (New York, 1935), p. 168.

35 Menachem Stern, *Greek and Latin Authors on Jews and Judaism* (Jerusalem, 1980), pp. 580–1.

36 Martin Goodman, 'The Roman State and the Jewish Patriarch in the Third Century', in *The Galilee in Late Antiquity*, ed. Lee I. Levine (Cambridge, Mass., 1992), pp. 127–59; Karl Strobel, 'Aspekte des politischen und sozialen Scheinbildes der rabbinischen Tradition: die spätere 2. und 3. Jhte. n. Chr.', *Klio* 72 (1990), pp. 478–97 at pp. 486–92.

37 Libanius, *Ep.* 973.2, Stern, p. 591.

38 Libanius, *Ep.* 974.2, Stern, p. 592.

39 Libanius, *Ep.* 1084.3, Stern, p. 593.

40 Libanius, *Ep.* 1105, Stern, p. 597. For similar relations between educated pagans and Christians in Egypt, see now R. S. Bagnall, *Egypt in Late Antiquity* (Princeton, NJ, 1993), p. 272.

41 These incidents are summarised in Brown, *Power and Persuasion*, pp. 71–115; the reader should know that they have been very differently interpreted by Ramsay MacMullen, 'The Social Role of the Masses in Late Antiquity', in *Changes in the Roman Empire: Essays in the Ordinary* (Princeton, NJ, 1990), pp. 250–76 and by Neil McLynn, 'Christian Controversy and Violence in the Fourth Century', *Kodai* 3 (1992), pp. 15–44.

42 E.g. Barbara Gassowska, 'Maternus Cynegius, Praefectus Praetorio Orientis and the Destruction of the Allat Temple in Palmyra', *Archeologia* 33 (1982), pp. 107–23.

43 Libanius, *Oratio*, 30, *On the Temples*, ed. and transl. A. F. Norman, *Libanius: Select Works 2*, Loeb Classical Library (Cambridge, Mass., 1977), pp. 92–150; on Callinicum, Ambrose, *Epp.* 40 and 41; at Panopolis, Shenoute, *Ep.* 24, ed. Leipoldt and Crum, pp. 79–84.

44 Libanius, *Oratio*, 30.9.

45 Libanius, *Oratio*, 30.12; Shenoute, *Ep.* 24, p. 79.16.

46 Callinicus, *Vita Hypatii* 33, transl. A. J. Festugière, *Les moines d'Orient* (Paris, 1961), II, p. 57.

47 Palladas, *Anthologia Palatina*, IX.528, ed. and transl. W. R. Paton, *The Greek Anthology*, Loeb Classical Library (Cambridge, Mass., 1968), 3.294.
48 Augustine, *Ep.* 50.
49 *Revue des études anciennes* 3 (1901), p. 273; F. Harmer, *Documents of the Ninth and Tenth Centuries* (Cambridge, 1914), pp. 13-15.

3 ARBITERS OF THE HOLY:
the Christian holy man in late antiquity

1 Barsanuphius, *Correspondance*, 91, transl. L. Regnault, *Barsanuphe et Jean de Gaza: Correspondance* (Solesmes, 1971), p. 84.
2 Barsanuphius, *Correspondance*, 569, transl. Regnault, p. 369.
3 *Vita Nicolai Sionitae*, 22, ed. I. and N. Ševčenko, *The Life of Nicholas of Sion* (Brookline, Mass., 1984), p. 43.
4 P. Brown, 'The Rise and Function of the Holy Man in Late Antiquity', *Journal of Roman Studies* 61 (1971), pp. 80-101, published in *Society and the Holy in Late Antiquity* (Berkeley, Calif., 1982); see also 'The Saint as Exemplar', *Representations* 1 (1983), pp. 1-25.
5 Augustine, *Confessions*, VI.13.23 and IX.4.12.
6 Barsanuphius, *Correspondance*, 771, transl. Regnault, p. 472.
7 Gregory of Tours, *Vita Patrum*, 10.1.
8 W. C. Till, 'Die koptischen Ostraka', *Österreichische Akademie der Wissenschaften, Phil.-Hist. Kl. Denkschrift*, 78.1 (Vienna, 1960), no. 261, p. 64.
9 Eustratius, *Vita Euthymii*, 58 and 60, *Patrologia Graeca*, 86.2340A and 2341C.
10 V. Turner and E. Turner, *Image and Pilgrimage in Christian Culture* (New York, 1978), p. 15.
11 Valerius of Bierzo, *Ordo Quaerimoniae*, 2.6 and 7.1; *Replicatio*, 13.3, ed. C. M. Aherne (Washington, DC, 1949), pp. 75 and 93; 143.
12 Gregory, *Dialogi*, II.8.1-4.
13 Y. Hirschfeld, *The Judaean Monasteries in the Byzantine World* (New Haven, Conn., 1992).
14 John of Ephesus, *Lives of the Eastern Saints*, 35, *Patrologia Orientalis*, 18, pp. 607-20; *Chronicon anonymum pseudo-Dionysianum*, transl. R. Hespel, *Corpus Scriptorum Christianorum Orientalium* 507, *Scriptores Syri*, 213 (Louvain, 1989), pp. 27-8.
15 Thomas of Marga, *Book of the Governors* v.17, transl. E. A. W. Budge (London, 1893), p. 563.
16 Brown, 'The Rise and Function of the Holy Man', p. 91.

17 *Vita Symeonis jun.* 96, ed. P. van den Ven, *La vie ancienne de S. Syméon le jeune*, Subsidia hagiographica 32 (Brussels, 1962), 1.74–5; I share the scepticism of van den Ven, *Vie ancienne*, 2.92–3. See W. Djobadze, *Archaeological Investigations in the Region West of Antioch-on-the-Orontes* (Wiesbaden, 1986), pp. 57–114.

18 Similar narratives concerning the wealth of modern Islamic holy men have been accurately observed by M. Gilsenan, *Recognizing Islam: Religion and Society in the Modern Arab World* (New York, 1982), pp. 102–3.

19 D. Frankfurter, 'Stylites as *phallobates*: Pillar Religions in Late Antique Syria', *Vigiliae Christianae* 44 (1990), pp. 168–98.

20 Theodoret, *Historia Religiosa*, 26.13, *Patrologia Graeca* 82.1476B.

21 *Vita Symeonis Syriace*, 61 and 63, transl. R. Doran, *The Lives of Simeon Stylites*, Cistercian Studies 112 (Kalamazoo, Mich., 1992), pp. 141 and 143, with the comments on pp. 22-3.

22 W. C. Till, *Koptische Heiligen- und Märtyrerlegende, pt. 2, Analecta Christiana Orientalia*, 108 (Rome, 1936), p. 65.

23 S. Kaplan, *The Monastic Holy Man and the Evangelization of Early Solomonic Ethiopia* (Wiesbaden, 1984), p. 115.

24 *Vita Theodori Syceotae* 37–8, ed. A. J. Festugière, *Vie de Théodore de Sykéon*, Subsidia hagiographica 48 (Brussels, 1970), pp. 32–4.

25 Gregory of Tours, *Vita Patrum*, 9.2.

26 J. Fentress and C. Wickham, *Social Memory* (Oxford, 1992), p. 51.

27 G. Dagron, 'Le saint, le savant, l'astrologue', in *Hagiographie, cultures et sociétés* (Paris, 1981), pp. 143–56, and now, especially, V. Déroche, 'Pourquoi écrivait-on des recueils de miracles? L'exemple des miracles de Saint Artémios', *Les saints et leurs sanctuaires: textes, images, et monuments*, Byzantina Sorbonensia 11 (Paris, 1993), pp. 95–116.

28 *Vita Petri Iberi*, ed. R. Raabe (Leipzig, 1895), p. 72.

29 *Miracula Ss. Cyri et Johannis* 28, *Patrologia Graeca*, 87.3504A.

30 *V. Theod. Syc.*, 4, ed. Festugière, p. 4; transl. E. Dawes and N. H. Baynes, *Three Byzantine Saints* (Oxford, 1948), pp. 88–9.

31 *V. Theod. Syc.*, 145, ed. Festugière, p. 114; Dawes and Baynes, p. 182.

32 Anastasius Sinaita, *Quaestiones* 94, *Patrologia Graeca*, 89.1733A.

33 Augustine, *Ep.* 11*.13, ed. Bibliothèque augustinienne 46B (Paris, 1987), pp. 206–8.

34 Barsanuphius, *Correspondance*, 416, transl. Regnault, p. 290.

35 Quodvultdeus, *Liber Promissionum*, vi.11, ed. R. Braun, Sources chrétiennes 102 (Paris, 1964), pp. 608–10.

36 *Vita Danielis*, 29, with A. J. Festugière, *Les moines d'Orient* (Paris, 1961), II, p. III, n. 41.

37 Gregory of Tours, *De gloria confessorum*, 77.
38 *Chronicon anon. pseudo-Dionysianum*, transl. Hespel, pp. 64-5 and 85.
39 John Rufus, *Plerophoriae*, 22 and 33, *Patrologia Orientalis*, 8, pp. 40 and 75; John Moschus, *Pratum Spirituale*, 186, *Patrologia Graeca*, 87.3065D.
40 Severus of Antioch, *Contra impium grammaticum*, III.9, transl. J. Lebon, *Corpus Scriptorum Christianorum Orientalium*, 102, *Script. Syri* 51 (Louvain, 1952), p. 181.
41 Athanasius, *Festal Letters*, ed. T. Lefort, *Corpus Scriptorum Christianorum Orientalium*, 150/151, *Script. Coptici* 19/20 (Louvain, 1955), pp. 65/45-7.
42 A. van Lantschoot, 'Fragments d'une homélie copte de Jean de Parallos', *Studi e Testi* 121 (1946), pp. 296-326.
43 Marinus, *Vita Procli*, 28.
44 Cyril of Scythopolis, *Vita Euthymii*, 25, transl. R. Price, *Lives of the Monks of Palestine by Cyril of Scythopolis*, Cistercian Studies 114 (Kalamazoo, Mich., 1991), pp. 34-5.
45 B. Flusin, *Miracle et histoire dans l'œuvre de Cyrille de Scythopolis* (Paris, 1983), pp. 126-8.
46 Doran, *Lives of Simeon Stylites*, pp. 43-5.
47 *V. Sym. auct. Antonio* 15 and Appendix 21, Doran, pp. 93 and 225.
48 *V. Sym. syr.* 79 and *V. Sym. auct. Ant.*, Appendix 25, Doran, pp. 161 and 227.
49 Cyril of Scythopolis, *Vita Sabae* 62, transl. Price, p. 173.
50 Besa, *Life of Shenoute* 102-5, transl. D. N. Bell, Cistercian Studies 73 (Kalamazoo, Mich., 1983); see F. Thélamon, *Païens et chrétiens* (Paris, 1981), p. 283.
51 *Discourse on the Compassion of God and of the Archangel Michael*, transl. E. A. W. Budge, *Coptic Texts in the Dialect of Upper Egypt* (London, 1915), pp. 757-8.

Index

Printed in the United States
By Bookmasters